# A Generous Community

# A GENEROUS COMMUNITY

## Being the Church in a New Missionary Age

## C. ANDREW DOYLE

Author of *Unabashedly Episcopalian*

Morehouse Publishing
NEW YORK

Unless otherwise noted, the Scripture quotations contained herein are from the New Revised Standard Version Bible, copyright © 1989 by the Division of Christian Education of the National Council of Churches of Christ in the U.S.A. Used by permission. All rights reserved.

Morehouse Publishing, 19 East 34th Street, New York, NY 10016

Morehouse Publishing is an imprint of Church Publishing Incorporated.

www.churchpublishing.org

Cover design by Laurie Klein Westhafer

Typeset by Denise Hoff

Library of Congress Cataloging-in-Publication Data

Doyle, C. Andrew.

A generous community: being the church in a new missionary age / C. Andrew Doyle.

    pages cm

    Includes bibliographical references.

ISBN 978-0-8192-3230-4 (pbk.)—ISBN 978-0-8192-3231-1 (ebook)
1. Church renewal. 2. Church renewal—Episcopal Church.
I. Title.

BV600.3.D69 2015

283'.73—dc23

Printed in the United States of America

# Contents

# Foreword

In the past, uniformity sold products. It still does in many sectors. For example, it still matters that every McDonald's hamburger is exactly the same.

Uniformity sold religions too. The fact that every Catholic mass was, for many centuries, in the same historic (and dead) language that few Catholics understood was a plus. It was only those rebel Protestants who stooped to read Scripture, pray, and worship in tawdry living languages like . . . English! Of course, eventually Catholics joined the vernacular club too.

But uniformity has its drawbacks. If you specialized in vinyl records in the Sixties or 8-tracks in the Seventies or cassettes in the Eighties or CDs in the Nineties, you made a lot of money. The same was true for products in the film and camera industry. Who could have guessed that a day would come when music would be played and photographs would be taken on . . . phones?

Religions face a similar challenge. Just as companies had to answer the question of whether they were in the record, 8-track, cassette, or CD business—or whether they were actually in the music dissemination business—religions have to grapple with what their true mission is: Gathering people to use a certain edition of a prayer book? Preparing clergy to fill vacancies in existing buildings? Convincing people to say certain creeds or transfer their money to the accounts of certain institutions?

Many religious leaders are loyal to the good old days when every church was more or less the same, when pastors or priests could be unplugged and transferred to another congregation like a module in a machine, when words like Presbyterian or Episcopal or Roman Catholic meant one thing and one thing only, when the church's liturgy was as predictable as a McDonald's cheeseburger.

God bless them.

Other religious leaders are saying something quite different. Others have learned to say: "We're not in the LP or CD business—we're in the music dissemination business," or "We're not in the camera and film business—we're in the image-sharing business," or "We're not in the stamp, envelope, and mailbox business—we're in the communication business," or "We're not in the hamburger business—we're in the nourishment and health business."

So these religious leaders are saying: "Beneath our traditions and conventional structures, there is something deeper running like a current, pulsing like a heartbeat . . . a mission, a calling, an adventure, a challenge, an opportunity. And that's what we're about. To pursue that deeper mission is what matters most to us, even if that means recycling some of our traditions and revolutionizing some of our conventional structures."

Bishop Andy Doyle is helping lead the way in refocusing on the deep current and spiritual heartbeat of Christianity. He is using his position in the Episcopal Church not to clamp down and impose uniformity, but to open up new possibilities and stimulate creativity. He knows that doing so will upset some people—especially those who are intimidated by changes in so many areas of society and who want their church to be *the one place in the world where everything stays exactly the same*! (They don't realize that what they're asking for is not a church but a museum. Or maybe a cemetery?)

He has written this book to help congregations face the challenge of change not simply as a necessary burden (like quitting cigarettes, maybe, or losing those fifteen pounds that somehow snuck onto your frame in recent years) but as a creative opportunity, vocation, and adventure.

The content of this book is transformational enough, but then add the resources for group interaction and you have a combination that—with your energetic engagement—can mean a brighter future for your church, your life, and the lives of your grandchildren's grandchildren.

So here's my hope: that you will read this book, and about halfway through, decide to form a reading group. Then you'll invite four to twenty of the most interesting, creative, and energetic people in your congregation to gather every week to discuss a chapter—maybe over a meal. Amazing things could happen!

Or maybe you're one of those people who is part of such a reading group. Bring all of your creativity and energy to a conversation about the future—of your church and of our world. Engage the questions, do the exercises. Amazing things could happen!

I expect that within a few paragraphs or pages, your imagination will start generating some truly exciting possibilities.

Brian D. McLaren

# Preface

A friend reminds me that publishing is like performing—it's never perfect. I am grateful for that reminder. *Church: A Generous Community Amplified for the Future* was fun to write. It is long and an in-depth look at our missional history as a church. Part of its imperfection lies in its inaccessibility to the person in the pews. This is the reason for *A Generous Community: Being the Church in the New Missionary Age*. This book is not perfect, but I had fun writing it and am glad to have had many individuals walk along the writing path with me as friends and companions. It is a distilled and tight text which offers a more accessible vision to the church. My prereaders have been honest when in my exuberance I was too strong. They let me know when my hope was too subtle. With friends and colleagues such as these, we will most assuredly steer our Church into the future faithfully.

The Rt. Rev. Neil Alexander reminded me of the movie *The Color of Money* and pool hustler Fast Eddy Felson (played by Paul Newman) who says, "Pool excellence is not about excellent pool. It's about becoming someone." This is true in book writing too. This book is about me becoming a better bishop from having thought and dreamed about the future. We will become a better diocese and a better Church from having had this conversation. We are always on the road to becoming the person and Church that God dreams.

I am grateful to conversation partners who, over the last two years, have helped me think about the future of the Church and how to take steps forward and march into it: Margaret Wheatley, Bob Johansen, and Rachel Hatch, among many others. Their own imagination and foresight have given me space in which to think and imagine. The result is two books with much in common but intended for different conversation partners. It is my hope that this book, A Generous Community: Being the Church in a New Missionary Age, will be used in congregations of the Episcopal Church and beyond to spur conversation about the role the local Christian community is called to fill, now and in the future. Its companion, Church: A Generous Community in an Amplified Age, is intended to help the leadership of church bodies, institutions, and seminaries understand the times in which we live and how we can act effectively in the future. Together these are valuable tools for the church as it sets sail into the sea of change which is ahead.

I am especially thankful to the Rev. John Newton, who wrote the discussion questions, reflections exercises, and suggestions for lectio divina that follow each chapter, as well as the guide to lectio divina in the appendix. His ability to help reflect on and lead people into formative action is a gift to the Church, my diocese, and to me.

I have many good friends who have been supportive during the writing of this book. There are three who deserve special mention. When I first publicly talked about the book, it was at a lunch with my friend John Price. I realize now his interest and encouragement enabled me to have that first bit of faith to continue the work of thinking and writing. As I neared the halfway mark, that place where all good books go to die, I had drinks with a new friend Matt Russell. It was Matt's excitement that encouraged me forward. Finally, as I worked on the footnotes, I realized that the two most important influences on my thinking are Daniel Kahneman and Nassim Nicholas Taleb. The Rev. Patrick Miller introduced me to both of these authors and their books. He also has been an excited conversation partner over the last year of writing, and for his support, encouragement, and excitement, I am thankful.

I was glad to have served on the Task Force for Re-Imagining the Church (TREC). It was a great gift to me to be placed in a room with committed leaders who believe we can do better as missionaries and that God is inviting us into a new future. It was an honor to serve and to work toward a common reimagined future together. The outcome of that discussion will be transformational for the Episcopal Church. Though this book is of my own thinking, it was helpful to be in conversation with others about the future as I was writing.

I want to say a special thank-you to Church Publishing and Richard Bass, my editor, who grabbed the vision of a book that would spur conversation about what our Church is, what it could become, and how we can help shape its future. Richard has been a faithful leader throughout the editing process. His vision for this book has sustained it over the last year.

In the summer of 2014, I was blessed by the Diocese of Texas to be provided a time to reflect about the future of our diocese and the Church. This book is the culmination of that time away. I enjoyed many days in the mountains of Colorado thanks to friends the Rev. Kit and Rufus Wallingford and their children, Halley and Thomas Ortiz. Janie and Jim Stevens were also gracious and giving during this time, providing a hide-away to be with family. Their generosity allowed my family to rest and enjoy the outdoors with me. I spent the mornings writing, enjoying coffee, and looking out at brilliant painted skies. I could not ask for any better environment in which to write.

I am so happy that JoAnne married me. She put up with me during the writing of the book—in fact it is her special talent to put up with me all the time. She has forever been and continues to be my first reader, something saved for only the ones I love. She is the one who inspires me by taking interest in my writing, life, and ministry. In 2015 we celebrate twenty-five years of marriage. Our two beautiful girls, a great group of close friends, and a wonderful life together reveal our happiness in having found one another.

For these blessings and all the blessings of this life, I am humbled and grateful.

# Introduction

On August 2, 2014, a large semi truck dropped off a gigantic dirt digger at the house across the street. Within fifteen minutes, it was destroying the 1960s ranch house that had most recently been the home of a series of renters. It is a scene familiar in Houston. Old homes, and just about anything that is left standing without purpose, is torn down so that a new something can be put up in its place. There is something that is both exciting and disturbing about this routine demolition. An architect friend once told me that not every house *should* be saved. Sometimes I think we think it is easier to simply discard the past and build a new thing.

I have discovered there is no real starting over. We are always walking into the future with a key ingredient of the past—ourselves. Lessons learned and lessons unlearned all come with us. The only thing new that is taken into the future is the lie that it is untouched and disconnected from all that comes before it. Bill Bryson, in his book *At Home*, writes, "Houses are amazingly complex repositories. What I found, to my great surprise, is that whatever happens in the world—whatever is discovered or created or bitterly fought over—eventually ends up, in one way or another, in your house. Wars, famines, the Industrial Revolution, the Enlightenment—they are all there in your sofas and chests of drawers, tucked into the folds of your curtains, in the downy softness of your pillows, in the paint on your walls and the water in your pipes."[1]

The same is true for the Church—God's house—in which we find ourselves. It is a storehouse of the past. It is filled with artifacts from the theology, liturgy, and Sunday Schools of our past. The culture has deposited here the Enlightenment, the Industrial Revolution, the 1950s, and all manner of musical tastes. If we take a walk and make our way through God's house, we will find some interesting truths about the past Church. If we look closer still, we will see the profound impact the last 200 years have had on who we think we are and how we use the buildings of our faith. Here is the fascinating part though: If we look closely and we look at the world around us, we will also see artifacts of the future.

This is a book about taking a second look at our Episcopal Church. It is about seeing a living organism making its way in the world in space and in time. This book is about the future and the Church's place in it. It is also about what will be necessary for us to remain and grow, and what can fall away. It is about our future mission, undertaken in stewardship, service, and evangelism. It is about taking up that work with excellence, unity, and connectivity.

What I am proposing is that a Christian community that is more diverse in mission, community size, economic model, service, and leadership makes us less fragile. For over five years, I have looked and listened for the exciting future that is already making itself known. As we walk around the Church and look out into the world around us, we can see it. We can hear the future calling to us to see, and take note.

I offer this book as a person tasked with casting a vision for my diocese and the wider Church. I offer it as a participant in its past and a leader of its future. I chair many Church boards, I am the head of several governance structures, and I am responsible for the livelihood of many clergy, professors, teachers, and lay professionals. Therefore, I am invested in the future of the Church and in helping it thrive. This means asking difficult questions that will most certainly bring difficult answers along the way.

My hope is that this book will get people talking, that it will start a conversation wherein people listen, critique, and prepare carefully for what is coming as it comes, remaining strong and focused in the meantime. We cannot bury our head in the sand. Instead we must work together with anticipation and with patience as we sort out the trends that will be manifest as time evolves. With this book in hand and brave conversation partners, I believe we can understand these trends and their role in our future mission.

This book is for all those who have lost hope in our Church over the last two decades and especially for those who deeply desire to be part of what God is doing in the world around us. Books do not make the future—people do. This book includes study questions to ponder and pray over. It includes bible studies and opportunities to engage the future Church. I hope you will join me in groups of five or six and become the church at work in the world. Grab this vision and join the thousands others like yourself who hope for a different church, a living church, a vibrant church, a transformed and transformative church.

I am here to tell you there is an exciting movement forward—into our future. True, the tide is one that draws us forever backwards toward the shore. Jesus, however, is in the boat ahead of us. He beckons to us. He invites us to put our backs into it, to beat against the past, and to come along. He invites us to join him and to make our way across to the other side with him. Only in following God in Christ Jesus into the future kingdom will we find our way onto the soil of that distant land. We must make our way from the past into the future, heads up, and eyes on Jesus. For it is there—on that distant shore—that Jesus is standing, waiting, with the fire burning. He stands there and he is eager to break bread with us and to hear stories of our passage.

# 1

......................................................................................................

# Schrödinger's Church

Do you believe in a dying Church? Or do you believe in a living, vibrant Church? I caution you to be careful how you answer; everything may depend on it. In most every field of study, the modern conundrum of how one sees the world is a debate that is alive and well.

Humans can look at the same thing and describe its behavior differently. For the scientific community this paradox is highlighted because, at the microscopic level, matter behaves differently from matter at the macroscopic level, or so it seems. What scientists see through a microscope and what they can see with the human eye tells them different things about how the universe works. This is the theory of *superposition*, also called the *observer's paradox:* the observation or measurement itself affects the outcome, and that outcome does not exist unless the measurement is made. This all can really make your brain hurt.

The dispute among scientists about how one sees the world began a long time ago. It began when Isaac Newton and his fellow physicist Christiaan Huygens proposed competing theories of light: light was thought either to consist of waves (Huygens) or of particles (Newton). The debate continued for hundreds of years. Albert Einstein and his

1

contemporary Erwin Schrödinger argued about it. Schrödinger eventually tweaked Einstein's theory in his own work, moving the discussion forward. Schrödinger was a physicist who was interested in offering a thought experiment that would illustrate the theory of superposition.[1] He wanted to show that the new quantum view of probabilities was stronger than his predecessor's views of the world as deterministic. He devised what today is a famous illustration of this principle. Schrödinger's theoretical experiment works this way: We place a living cat (forever to be known as Schrödinger's cat) into a steel chamber, along with a device containing a vial of hydrocyanic acid—a radioactive substance. When a single atom of the substance decays during the test period, a relay mechanism will trip a hammer, which will, in turn, break the vial and kill the cat. We know that it will decay; we just don't know when.

What the experiment illustrates is that the observer cannot know whether or not an atom of the substance has decayed yet, and consequently, cannot know whether the vial has been broken, the hydrocyanic acid released, and the cat killed. Since we cannot know, according to quantum law, the cat is considered both dead and alive, in what is called a superposition of states. There are yet to be discovered many probabilities, and we will participate in them, shaping them and forming them. When we break open the box and learn the condition of the cat, the superposition is lost, and the cat becomes one or the other (dead or alive).[2] The probabilities are shown to be true. This is of course an oversimplification of the experiment, but I believe you understand my point. Please note there was no actual cat, and no cats were harmed in the thought experiment in Schrödinger's brain.

Margaret Wheatley, in her book *Leadership and the New Science: Discovering Order in a Chaotic World*, says it this way: "Reality is co-created by our process of observation," and "we participate in the creation of everything we observe."[3] Two realities are always in existence within a thing, and how we observe or what we say about a thing changes the essence of it. How we look at Schrödinger's cat actually shapes its fate, whether it lives or dies. In fact, more than two realities may exist together at the same time. In quantum theory, it is recognized that in any given moment two states exist and that the observer shapes the reality of that which is observed. This is true for art and people. This is true for light. This is true for Schrödinger's cat. And, it is true for the Church. How you see your Church has a direct effect on the Church itself.

The Church that we observe is very much the Church that comes into being. If we observe a Church that is dying, then we will most assuredly add to growing entropy. If we observe a Church that is alive and thriving, then our Church will thrive and be alive. This is not simply a power-of-positive-thinking lesson. Quantum physics teaches us that the observer shapes the reality of that being observed.

In the Church, we call that the power of the Living Word. In the same way that God creates by speaking his Word, we too cocreate (although on a much smaller scale) our Church and the world around us by how we perceive it and the kinds of stories we tell about it. The implication, I think, is that nothing is more threatening to the life and mission of the Church than cynical and negative leadership. The inability to see God's hand at work in the world around us creates an environment where it gets harder and harder to see God. Life in ministry then becomes a downward spiral.

And so how we see and what we say about ourselves and the Church matters greatly. Theologian Paul Zahl once said, "We become as we are regarded."[4] These quantum thinkers are helpful: reality is cocreated by our process of observation. How we observe the Church will create the Church we observe.

This is, of course, not the first time we have been offered an opportunity to think about this. There is a story in the Bible that goes like this . . . Jesus has been teaching and he is probably tired. So, he decides to get away for a bit. He and his friends—Peter, James, and John—take some time away from the crowds of people and the daily routine of teaching and healing. They go to the top of a mountain to pray. While Jesus is praying and the others are watching, Jesus begins to be changed. His face changes and shines bright. His clothes become dazzling white. "Wow," they think, "this is really awesome." Then two great prophets appear: Moses and Elijah. They are as wild-looking as Jesus—sparkly and white. They are all there and they are talking about everything that is about to happen and how Jerusalem is going to be an important place in the story of Jesus. It is a glorious moment.

Peter says to Jesus, "It is good for us to see this and to be here with you." Then Peter says, "Let us make three dwellings, three booths, three boxes in which we can have you and Moses and Elijah dwell. It will be great because then people can come to the mountain like we did and be here with you." But Jesus doesn't accept their plan. Jesus is clear that their business is to leave the mountaintop and get back to the world, preaching, teaching, and healing. This is the work of Jesus, and he is clear that this is the work of those who follow him (Luke 9:28–36).

The story is dynamic and about a living mission. It is about being alive and in the world and not crammed into a box. It is a story about abundant life and abundant mission. I believe in a Church that is alive and flourishing in the world, that is ancient and new, multiplying and diverse, creative, and so much more. This book is about the Church that I believe in. It is Schrödinger's Church with all its paradoxes and complexity. It is the Church I observe and believe is possible in a new missionary age, a generous community united in service and mission.

It is our work to make this Church. Certainly God is even now creating this Church, and God's Holy Spirit is moving to bring it to completion. Yet we are the makers. We are the cocreators. What will it look like? How will it exist in the world? What will its mission look like? Who will lead it? How will it be organized? These are important questions to ask if we are the makers, with God, of this endeavor. Regardless of the form that this missionary Church takes, from the outset it is important to remember the words of King Solomon regarding the temple: "The highest heaven cannot contain you, much less this house that I have built!" (I Kings 8:27).

It is clear to me that we have a desire to make things and to build things. It is part of who we are. We are going to continue to build machines like we have always done, but we also are going to be invested in building communities and networks. We will forever be about the work of cocreating by taking those things available to us and making something new from them, tinkering with or repurposing parts from already existing things. We are in the end made to make. This reality is now making its presence known throughout the world through the maker movement. This movement has a motto: *If you can't open it, then you don't own it.*

The idea is that if you can't open it and take it apart and use it and reuse it, then you really don't own it. It is somebody else's. Let me give you an example from a company I am closely connected with, Apple. I love Apple products, so that is my disclaimer. If you by chance own any kind of smartphone—but especially the iPhone—you've bought it and you own it, or so you think. But you can't unlock it, and you can't use unapproved things on it. You can only use the things that Apple says you can use. Now some of you are probably more technical than I am and know how to unlock or "jailbreak" your iPhone, but for me—the poor iPhone owner, who does not know these things—I am fearful that if I unlock my phone, I will void the warranty. My phone's ultimate potential is closed to me. I own it . . . but I don't own it. And there it is. I am a user. This is an amazing thing, given that Apple itself is one of the founding parents of the maker movement in computer technology.

Here's another example. Every year since 2006, a makers' conference called the Maker Faire has been held, and all these creative types come from all over the world, and they gather, and they show off their innovations. There's art and new technology, and everything is open and reusable. A number of years ago, some artists came up with the idea of dropping a Mentos candy into a one-liter bottle of Diet Coke. Those of you who have teenage boys may have seen this already. Or you can go on the Internet and watch it in action. Even better, you can do this in your own backyard. When you drop the Mentos into the bottle, it creates a chemical reaction with the Diet Coke. It explodes, and geysers of Diet Coke shoot out of the top. Some Maker Faire artists were going around and capturing images of explosions as a form of art. Now, you and I can debate whether that is art or not, but that's not the point of this illustration. Here is the rest of the story. Mentos and Coca-Cola did not like this, because their products weren't intended for this; they were invested in a closed use of their products. They apparently intended to sue these artists to keep them from repurposing their product. Evidently, a groundswell of sixth graders all over the country stood up to them and said, "No." As the story goes, they begrudgingly gave in. Today both Mentos and Coca-Cola sponsor these artists at the Maker Faire. What the companies had to come to terms with was that they could not control their products and that they were open to new applications or repurposing.[5]

There is a passage in Mark's Gospel where the disciples get grumpy about people bringing their children to Jesus. In their opinion these children are really messing up the gospel. These children are a problem to the disciples, who obviously are Very Serious Men. "There is no time for this," they thought. They decide that they are going to keep the children from coming to Jesus, because they are interrupting all the other really good work Jesus is doing. So, they say, "Look. We think the little ones should all go away. They can't be here." Scholars have taught us that the first followers of Jesus were called the "Little Ones," which helps us understand the meaning of the text. As we ponder what the disciples are doing, it becomes clear that they are invested in a closed system. They want to control how Jesus is used, how Jesus relates, with whom Jesus spends time, and who has access to Jesus. Who they think should have access to God is impacted by their desire for control. It is not the first nor the last time in the Scriptures that the disciples will think that they are able to control the good news of salvation and manage Jesus. But Jesus tells them, "Let the little children come to me, and do not stop them; for it is to such as these that the kingdom of heaven belongs" (Matt. 19:14).

Jesus is going around opening up the kingdom to whoever would listen. In fact, that seems to be the purpose of his coming. He has come to glorify God, bring good news, and open up and give access to the reign of God for all people. This must have driven the disciples nuts! Just as they are figuring things out, creating a new power structure, and getting clarity on the best way to market the rock star Jesus . . . he is going around handing out backstage passes to everyone. The reign of God is open to everyone.

The God that we choose to follow is a God who is out and among the people. The God we follow bids us make a Church that is where he is. We are to make a Church that is out and among the people. Like God we are to make room for creativity and innovation. This God cannot be contained. God's mission cannot be contained. God's mission has a Church and that Church is not to contain God.

The Church must repurpose; it must remake itself into a new creation so that God may once again be accessed through its ministry. The Church is a handmade vessel of God's grace. It can no longer choose to be a stumbling block for those who long for a little measure of grace, mercy, and kindness in a world that is often cold and dark. The Church must choose to take a step forward to find this God. Where the Church is in the way, it must change. We must allow people to come forward and find God, whether it is through the church doors or to sit and listen to somebody out in the world.

For many of us, access to God and God's love is why we are in the Church. We belong because it makes a difference in our lives. It changes who we are. It challenges us to be a better people. Such a God cannot be contained, even in you.

We must become a generation of church-makers who play in the waters of baptism and in the Scriptures and around God's altar. This is sacred and holy play through which we reenact—inside and outside church buildings, and in our lives—the great story of God's creation.

We are to be about making the world into a different place. We are to make it different with all the tools at our disposal. Most especially we are to make it new with God's love, grace, forgiveness, and mercy. We are to share and open up our church and walk out into the sweet-smelling and lush garden of creation. We are to invite, welcome, and connect with others. We are to share the message that God says to all people—"Come unto me all you who travail and are heavy laden and I will refresh you." God says to us who are weighed down by the world, "Come unto me. I'll give you rest." Don't keep the little children away. Don't keep away those who have tried to follow Jesus and believe they have failed. Don't keep those who have drifted away from church from God. Give God away. By all means let them all come. And let us go. And let us make the Church together.

## Discussion Questions

1. Bishop Doyle says that "nothing is more threatening to the life and mission of the Church than cynical and negative leadership." What specific practices can we undertake in order to become more hopeful and expectant leaders?

2. What aspects of the Church need to be repurposed? What will this "repurposing" require?

3. Do you believe we are born with a maker instinct? What does it mean to say that we are cocreators with God?

4. Think of all the ways in which the Church is already creative and innovative. How might we build on these strengths?

5. Bishop Doyle asserts that "how we observe the Church will create the church we observe." Can you think of a specific example of how this is true?

## Spiritual Exercise

Make a list of all the negative words you have heard used to describe the Church. After making the list, prayerfully read Ephesians 1:3–14. Now make a second list with the words this passage uses to describe the Church. Ponder how your experience of ministry and mission might change if you and others at your congregation saw the Church as Ephesians describes it.

*Suggested Passage for Lectio Divina:* Mark 10:46–52

## Suggested Reading

Bob Johansen, *Leaders Make the Future: Ten New Leadership Skills for an Uncertain World*. San Francisco: Berrett-Koehler, 2012.

Margaret Wheatley, *Leadership and the New Science: Discovering Order in a Chaotic World*. San Francisco: Berrett-Koehler, 2006.

# 2

# A New Missionary Age

The Lemhi Pass is at the border of Montana and Idaho. A wooden fence, cattle-guard crossing, and logging road mark the spot. One arrives there by following the Missouri River from Fort Benton to Fort Peck Lake along the Lolo Trail. When you stand there now, it looks in many ways as it looked on the morning of August 12, 1805, when, with friends nearby, a man made his way to the top. That moment is described clearly in his journal: "We proceeded on the top of the dividing ridge from which I discovered immense ranges of high mountains still to the West of us with their tops partially covered with snow." The man, Meriwether Lewis, was the first European American to look on the great northwestern range, the first to take a step out of the Louisiana Territory onto the western side of the Continental Divide.[1]

For Lewis, we can imagine that the sight suggested two great worlds colliding. Two thoughts occurring simultaneously, neither fully formed.

With the disheartening sight, the first thought would be "the shock, the surprise," as historian John Logan Allen mused, "For from the top of that ridge were to be seen neither the great river that had been promised nor the open plains extending to the shores of the South Sea . . . the geography of hope [gave way] to the geography of reality."[2] The journey to find a western portage to travel by boat from east to west across the United States was a failure. Everything Lewis was certain he would find not only was *not there*—it never would be. The dream, framed by a year of study and preparation and two years of travel across wild country, was over.

The second thought was a reaction to the view of the great empire of the Americas. Encircled by a grand panorama, Lewis could envision a wealthy and abundant new territory. Little had changed in transportation, energy, and food since the Greeks, but Meriwether Lewis glimpsed in its raw form the bountiful nation we were destined to become. He could not, however, imagine what it would take to unify the land, nor could he predict the tragic saga of tribal relationships that would be left in the wake of these efforts.[3]

These two thoughts—the immensity of the task and the enormity of the opportunity—shifted our understanding of the land we occupy and shaped who Americans are today. Today we are again becoming a new people, transformed and forged in a furnace of sweeping change. Not unlike on that August 1805 morning, America's social and economic geography is giving way beneath our feet. The past falls away in the present, while the future is yet to solidify. Our time requires clear vision and the ability to see beyond the chaos and incongruities of our time to a future others cannot see. If we look carefully, we may see the future God hopes for us.

# A VUCA World

Bob Johansen of the Institute for the Future (IFTF) reminds us that we live in a world fraught with volatility, uncertainty, complexity, and ambiguity (VUCA).[4] As a church, we have a nagging knowledge that things are not as they were. We have acted out of an understanding that if we simply did things better, all would return to normal. We have consistently and stubbornly believed that:

- those who are called by God to be Episcopalians will find the Episcopal Church and walk through its doors
- once they are inside the doors, they will stay because of the awesome liturgy

- one day we will grow again, and then we can take care of our deferred maintenance
- all we need is the right clergyperson and everything will be okay
- by solving the issue of the day, we would surge in growth
- clinging to the past, we await our revival

But that will not happen. Things have changed. *When* it all changed is unknowable. The Church is a complex organism that is rooted in geography, cultural contexts, and political worlds. Change was not the result of any one event, nor did it happen at one particular time. We must, however, admit that we have not been good at keeping up with this evolution. It crept in and is upon us, though we cannot yet fully comprehend its impact or what outcome it will bring.

We operate out of a model that depends upon assumptions about the culture that date to the middle of the last century of the last millennium: They will come, they will bring their family, and they will bring their money. For many congregations the simple battle against inflation will create a never-ending cost-cutting habit that will eventually put them out of business. We are holding on to an economically unsustainable model. The average congregation in the Episcopal Church hosts fewer than sixty people on any given Sunday. If a congregation was fortunate enough to have had wealthy benefactors, it may still be able to afford a full-time, seminary-trained rector. Reduced returns on investments because of a weakened economy, however, have forced hard choices about funding.

No longer does the Church corner the market on community life, networking, social services, weddings, funerals, or health care. Social media networks, bars, gyms, sports clubs, funeral homes, hospitals, and friends outperform us. Fewer people seek out and react positively to the Church's business-as-usual demeanor.

Everything has changed, but the Church idea has not. The Church did not have much to do with bringing the change, and it is similarly unable to stop it. People who gave a lifetime of faithful service and faithful ministry to the Church find in their last years that the Church can neither pastor nor bury them. Churches are closing, and people are forced to look elsewhere for support. This leads only to greater loss, conflict, and closures. If left unchecked, the demise will be painful and sad.

In the 1990s, the military began to use the term VUCA—volatility, uncertainty, complexity, and ambiguity—to describe the emerging world of the new millennium.[5] Bob Johansen has subsequently used the term to describe the complicated way in which the world comes into contact with corporations and communities.[6] Johansen has been interested in how these organizations make sense of the world and make their way through it. As we think about and ponder each element, it is possible for us to see how our own church systems work and how we are constantly reacting to the forces at work in the world around us.

## Volatility

Volatility is clearly present in the world. Let us pause for a moment and consider the acceleration of change. The immense growth in technology has within a short time changed the ways in which individuals communicate. Today we see that communication travels the globe immediately and creates innumerable reactions. News of Christian troubles a world away can now be the topic of local conversations within minutes. On Sunday mornings a priest can be faced with questions spanning the horizon from local gossip to global politics—both church and secular. A parishioner may well have reactions, both positive and negative, to events that only ten years ago would have gone unnoticed. Whatever the news, and wherever it originates, church life is impacted and faced with the need to respond to the growing chaos of local and global cultures. Volatility is part of our common experience in congregational church life.

## Uncertainty

Uncertainty is also a key factor that affects the life of the church. Predictability has long ceased to be a static value within the culture, our communities, and the local church. In the last four decades alone there has been a great deal of change. From prayer book revision to the blessing of same-gender relationships, the Church has been trying to figure out how to speak the language and engage in the cultural context that surrounds it. The resulting uncertainty about who the Church is and where it stands has sometimes resulted in conflicts that have led to take-it-or-leave-it standoffs.

Uncertainty is felt on Sunday morning as well. As individuals, we are energized by change and the excitement of discovery; at the same time, we long for some stability. This longing has meant that Sunday morning has grown into an even more segregated day when people huddle in like-minded silos, thinking they are safe from the uncertain world around them. No mainline denomination has been untouched by the results of congregations living in these uncertain times.

## Complexity

Complexity is the rule of the day. The closer we look, the more complex everything gets. What was true as quantum physics wrestled with the Newtonian worldview is present in every part of our culture. Not even the church escapes the widening consensus that we are a complex organic community. This is most obvious in the results of the Decade of Evangelism in the 1990s. Most everyone will say that this missionary effort was a failure, but I doubt those who found the Episcopal Church during the nineties would say that. What is a fact is that we now know that voting on a resolution calling for evangelism and tinkering with church structures will not lead to growth.

Today, after two decades of trying the quick fix, the church is waking up to admit that each congregation, each diocese, and the wider church is more complex and organic in its life than ever imagined. We have more questions today than we do answers. Ministry is the art of nurturing the ability to see a path through a maze of competing priorities. The complex nature of the world around us, our families, and our communities results in our path looking more like a sailboat tacking across an open sea than the directions from an accurate GPS device.

## Ambiguity

The first three elements of the VUCA world lead to the last one: ambiguity. Clergy wonder what is real anymore. Is a parishioner there to support you or get you kicked out? Your numbers are down, but the community is exploring the Bible more deeply than ever before. You are reaching out and engaging your community and meeting needs unaddressed for years, but not everyone cares. Clergy care a lot, and they want to be relevant.

The people in the pews want to do good work and find meaning in the midst of life. But there is a lot of confusion out there about what is valuable and what is not. There are a lot of mixed signals and confusing messages being sent by the preacher from the pulpit and by the church to the world. Competing truths and competing for members has become the theme of a new-millennium Christianity. Christianity today is literally consuming itself. Individuals throughout the world are trying to make a pilgrimage of meaning and find a bit of truth, but instead they find in us a bickering community of self-interested and inwardly focused individuals. We have, as a Christian faith, attempted to offer our version of a competing truth in the hopes of finding followers, instead of helping people live with the nature of today's new world. The church at large needs to become a better companion to those along the way.

## A Collision of Worldviews

We are living in a time when two worldviews are colliding: the world of Newtonian physics and the world of quantum physics. The tug and pull between these two worlds is what makes it so difficult to lead a church today. While we have glimpses of the future Church, we are stuck in the present with the church of the past. We have struggled with a church organization that is based upon the finest science of the eighteenth century.[7]

Most individuals make a living within a corporation that works on principles found in Newton's worldview. If you have ever had your organization described as a set of interlocking cogs, then you know exactly what I am talking about. Newtonian physics describes how the macro universe works. It describes how big bodies and machinery, planets and stars, missiles and spaceships work.[8] When I was nine years old, I checked out a book from the library on scientists. Today I realize the book was about Newtonian physicists; Isaac Newton, Johannes Kepler, and Galileo are the Newtonian physicists I grew up with. Their laws work well as long as what is being examined is large. When the details in need of examination get small, then quantum physics is necessary. Things that are complex and move fast seemingly require a different set of rules to measure and understand how they work. Most of our organizations, which operate on the Newtonian model, are not able to deal with the complexity of the minute forces that are bombarding and creating fields of influence and causing unexpected results. The church is no different.

The church analyzes its life and ministry by breaking it into large manageable ministry areas. We believe that if we control this area or make a seemingly major change, we will directly have a positive impact on the organization. We plan ministry and objectives with the idea that the world will respond in the anticipated manner. We believe that if the church can simply figure out the correct tools by which to measure reality, we can adjust to that reality and make everything right.

A great example of this is the Episcopal Church's governance structure. Some of the same individuals that influenced the framers of the then embryonic Episcopal Church influenced the framers of the Constitution. The designers of our Episcopal Church applied their understanding of Newtonian mechanics to institutional life, as did those in federal government, industry, and societies. I can imagine that the idea of individuals operating in synchronicity like a well-oiled machine was an exciting prospect. And it kind of worked for over two hundred years.

## VUCA Goes to Church

What happened? VUCA. The global explosion of communications and interrelated economies would bring chaos and, with it, volatility, uncertainty, complexity, and ambiguity. As Thomas Friedman would teach us all in a brief history of the twentieth century, the world is flat and we are all connected.[9] Jim Dator describes the effect this had on organizations in this way: "What happened in the twentieth century is that a new cosmology called quantum physics—and the new technologies of the electronic information and communications revolution—became out of sync with many social institutions and practices, specifically with government systems, which are still locked into technologies of two hundred years ago."[10]

We are aware of these shifts and of the inefficiencies of our church organization to navigate the chaotic world. For nearly two decades, the reality of our predicament has made its way into our conversations as a church. Though we have not known quite what to do with the information, we are aware that things are not well.

We are aware that the number of churches and people in them has not kept up with population growth. In fact, the number of individuals who don't go to church has more than doubled in two decades. The notion that young adults will return to church after college and marriage has become the reality that they don't. According to the Barna Group, the number of people who are completely unattached—having not attended church in the past year—equals one in four Americans.[11]

We also know that things in our culture are affecting the ability of small congregations to remain economically viable. There have been real economic pressures simply based on the cost of doing business; these are multiplied if we consider shrinking attendance. The economic change has affected most of our congregations. Consider for a moment that the average

Episcopal congregation hosts fewer than sixty on any given Sunday with an annual budget of around $80,000 to $100,000. The cost of electricity, water, and sewage alone has increased over the last three decades. The cost of gas and insurance for the priest's car has increased. The cost of telephone or mobile phone connectivity has increased. A truly fortunate congregation of fewer than sixty on a Sunday can afford a full-time person; however, that is rare indeed. In the end, the average congregation has to have a new member, who gives more than the average pledge as soon as he or she walks in the door, added to their communicant list every year in order to keep up with inflation alone. Even more unlikely, given the age of many parishioners, they can never lose a parishioner. It is an untenable economic reality that will continue to lead to the closure of small congregations.

Clergy are retiring in large numbers, and in some places there is a shortage of clergy. Quality of preaching and teaching is an issue, and finding the best people to lead communities is a challenge. Geographically, clergy move to where the jobs are—meaning one area may have too many and another not enough. The growth of alternative seminary schools training bivocational priests is an illustration of how the church is seeking to meet the pastoral needs in an economically challenged era. "Tentmakers" are currently helping to keep many congregations open.[12]

Churches have a cross section of generations, all of whom have different ideas about the church. Each generation is continuing to grow and to have new ideas. Each generation is responding in its own unique way to the cultural changes affecting the church. Personal stories and life events affect how they interpret both the culture and the church's response. Some of the loudest voices echo a refrain that the church is dying. Others are not sure but skeptically maintain a hopeless vision of the future. It is a false prophetic voice that echoes throughout every church, mainline and nondenominational, and the voice sounds like this: "If we don't (fill in the blank), our church will die." You can fill in the blank with the following: return to traditional values, commit to progressive ideals, use guitars, get rid of the hymnal, use more vestments, use no vestments, etc. The problem is that each suggestion echoes the Newtonian mechanized view of church ministry: If we replace the broken cog, we can get the machine started again. Such ideas lack an understanding that cultural volatility affects everything, including our mission. It denies the uncertainty that the action will be able to affect what are uncertain and unpredictable responses by a discriminating community. It ignores the complexity of the world and the interrelation of all things from liturgy to community life, to neighborhood, to connections, to message, and back again. And lastly, it does not consider the ambiguous and fickle nature of a quick-moving, trend-based culture.

And yet, the Church is a resilient organization. It lives because God has a mission and God's mission has a church.[13] Our theology teaches us that the church is the earthly vessel of the Holy Spirit. God is continually making and remaking the church as it navigates history. The church is made up of people, though, and we must ask ourselves if we are willing to be made well and figure out what God is doing. Sometimes it can be difficult to understand what God is doing because we are so tied to our understanding of the past.

In the Gospel of John, chapter 5, the author describes a festival and how Jesus and his disciples are drawn to Jerusalem. There is in Jerusalem a gate and by the gate, a pool. Along the edge of the pool are these little porticoes, and in them are blind, lame, and paralyzed people. The pool is a bubbling pool believed to have healing properties. So each time the water is stirred up, the ill and infirm make their way into the water in order to enjoy its healing properties. As Jesus is passing by, he encounters a man who has been there for thirty-eight years—thirty-eight years of hoping for healing, thirty-eight years of trying to make it to the pool, thirty-eight years of infirmity, thirty-eight years of paralysis. Jesus sees this man and he goes to him and asks, "Do you want to be made well?"

The man then gives a long list of reasons why this is not possible. "I don't have people to help me get to the pool. People knock me down just when I am about to make it. There are always people ahead of me with better skills." Jesus says, "Stand up, take your mat and walk." Of course, the religious leaders of the day say, "What? You can't heal on the Sabbath! We have rules." It's too late, the man is healed, he takes up his mat, and he walks. This is one of the important stories in John's Gospel, because it illustrates how the case against Jesus was made that he just wasn't religious enough; he just didn't quite get how things were done.

I always wonder if the man really wanted to be healed. He was so stuck. He was so sure he would be sick forever. He believed all the cards were stacked against him. He had no way of improving and lots of reasons why it wasn't worth trying. The religious authorities wanted to control the healing powers and wanted to make sure that it was clear you couldn't simply go around doing whatever you want; there is a form and a way and a means by which God works. Jesus proved both the man and the authorities wrong.

God is alive, and the Holy Spirit is moving and making all things new. The church is not to die, nor is it to be ill forever. Even now the Holy Spirit is troubling the waters, Jesus is coming near, and the opportunity for health is before us. The question is a good one. On this day, in this hour, cost what it will, do you want to be healed? I hope the answer for the church and the religious leaders of our generation is "Yes" (John 5:1–18).

## Discussion Questions

1. Meriwether Lewis was both disheartened and excited to realize that what he expected to find was a myth. In what way is Lewis's experience a metaphor for your own experience of Church? What disheartens you about the Church in today's world? What excites you?
2. Bishop Doyle writes, "No longer does the Church corner the market on community life, networking, social services, weddings, funerals, or health care." In the VUCA world, what *should* the Church "corner the market" on?
3. To adapt to the VUCA world, what must the Church give up? What must the Church take on?
4. When have you opted for a "quick fix" solution at your church? Did it work? What might a more "quantum" solution have entailed?
5. What leadership trait do you believe to be most important to church leadership in the VUCA world and why?

## Spiritual Exercise

Find a news article that captures your attention. Read the article and circle all the words that speak to the volatility, uncertainty, complexity, and ambiguity of our world. After doing so, write a brief reflection around the following questions. How is my congregation unprepared to meet the challenges this article poses? How is my congregation uniquely equipped to meet the challenges this articles poses?

*Suggested Passage for Lectio Divina:* John 5:1–9

# Suggested Reading

John Flowers and Karen Vannoy, *Adapt to Thrive*. Nashville: Abingdon Press, 2014.

Dwight J. Zscheile. *The Agile Church: Spirit-Led Innovation in an Uncertain Age*. New York: Morehouse, 2014.

# 3

......................................................................................................

# A Courageous Church

Is our Church worthy?

I think that members of the Episcopal Church, and members of most mainline denominations, don't feel worthy because their church is shrinking in number, takes stands that embarrass them (both conservative and liberal), changes its liturgy, won't change its liturgy—the list can go on and on. At the end of the day many of our members feel shame because their self-worth is tied up in these things—these ideas about church.[1]

## The Power of Shame

When our self-worth is tied to our church and people don't respond positively to it, we are are less inclined to offer it to others. We are crushed when people make fun of our church, tease us about our church, speak hatefully about our church, and don't honor it like we do. So we shut down. As researcher, social worker, and professor Brené Brown says, "You shut down. Shame tells you that you shouldn't have even tried. Shame tells you that you're not good enough and you should have known better . . . . You're officially a prisoner of 'pleasing, performing, and perfecting.'"[2]

The honest truth is that our church culture participates in this imprisonment and we have become good at the art of sharing shame. We train people that God wants only perfection and loves only perfection. We tell people they are not good enough and no offering will ever be pleasing to God. We have used shame to manipulate the culture wars and our churches' participation in them. We have shamed those who don't follow the religious traditions we hold dear. And others shame us for following the religious traditions they don't hold dear. Both traditions are shamed. We react to the VUCA world by feeling shame because we are no longer the strong and powerful Episcopal Church of the past.

But shame is not the gospel story. God chooses us in our imperfection. God reaches out and loves us before we repent. God offers grace and mercy to the sinner. The whole of the gospel story is about Christ Jesus, who comes into the world to draw the world closer to a living, loving God, whose message is not for the ones who have it right, but rather for the ones who don't get it at all. Jesus comes to share food with the hungry. He offers love for the unlovable. He befriends the friendless. He spends time and eats dinner with the outcasts. He heals the broken and lame. He spends almost all of his time with those who have received more than their share of shame, and he offers them love and courage and hope. In the end Jesus risks his life for the sake of the unlovable and dies at the hands of the righteous.

The church must reinvest itself in a new era of community making. The future Church will be focused on making communities that are filled with individuals who understand their worth is greater than the things of this world. Their worth is their very being, because they have been given life and breath from God. We are God's; we are all God's. This knowledge gives us strength and courage in the face of shame. These new communities and the people who inhabit them will dwell in the assurance that self-worth is tied to God and his love and mercy.

In order to navigate the world and deal with our own shame, we must begin by recognizing that it is actually the shame that is killing us. Shame undermines all innovation. When leaders hold back and don't risk a new idea because we have never done it that way before, we are experiencing shame control. When we are not honest with one another and don't help others improve with honest and loving feedback, shame is at work. The fear of believing we don't know enough to be a minister for Christ is shame. The inability to participate in making our communities healthy by our own participation is shame controlling the direction of our labors.

Our eucharistic prayer says that Christ's work makes us worthy to stand before God; not feeling worthy to stand before God is shame at work. Not speaking to others about the faith that is in us for fear of what people might think is shame silencing us.[3] So much of what passes for Christian community today participates in a shame culture. This culture of fear keeps us from embracing the new missionary age. Peter Sheahan, CEO of ChangeLabs, says, "Shame becomes fear, fear leads to risk aversion. Risk aversion kills innovation."[4] A lack of innovation is like spending thirty-eight years at the edge of a pool, hoping someone will help you in, hoping people will get out of your way, waiting for a miracle.

Jesus Christ risks; he offers himself to others, no matter what the stumbling blocks are ahead of him. In Christ we see ourselves differently. We see ourselves as people who are worthy and inspired to vulnerability. In Christ we are willing to be creative and innovative. We will try and try again. This is the way of Jesus. Brené Brown writes, "Shame keeps us small, resentful, and afraid. In shame-prone cultures, where parents, leaders, and administrators consciously or unconsciously encourage people to connect their self-worth to what they produce, I see disengagement, blame, gossip, stagnation, favoritism, and a total dearth of creativity and innovation."[5] Yikes! I want to be part of a community that is open and offers itself to the world and to all kinds of people from all backgrounds. I want to be part of a Church that takes risks for the good news of freedom that is found in Christ. I want to be part of a community that sees stumbling blocks as challenges to be overcome and presses on. I want to personally risk more, be more connected to other people, and as my grandmother used to say, "Resolve well, and persevere." This is a great vision for the Church and for the people in it. I believe it is the vision of God and the vision of Christ Jesus. I believe it was the vision that Christ had upon his crucifixion, in a hope that among the many things that might be laid to rest on the cross, shame would be chief among them. Let us lay our burden down and bravely face the future.

## The Church in Diaspora

Recently the term *diaspora* has been used to describe communities that exist in the culture of the new millennium. These communities are dispersed across the land like islands. The Christian Church is a large global web of scattered communities, islands in the sea of a culture that is quickly forgetting them. From large denominations to small nondenominational churches, we recognize that the world inside the church doors is vastly different from the world outside.

You might remember what I said earlier about how the observer influences the thing studied and the nature of Schrödinger's cat. This is true when it comes to these islands of church life and the castaways who dwell inside. The Church is a diaspora community. It is a community that shares values and worldviews. Inside a diaspora community, things are clear. It is clear who you are, what you stand for, and who you are not.[6] The Christian community, large and small, is primarily inwardly focused. Our communities are so unlike the rest of the world that it is difficult for people to look in and understand what we are doing and why. Things just don't make sense when you look out, and things don't make sense when you look in.[7] Your worldview determines how the community lives and moves and has its being within the larger society.

I believe that right now, in large part because of the shame factor, the Christian Church has become an unhealthy diaspora. We categorize people in such a way as to shame those not like ourselves. We put people into definable groups and navigate our relationships by who has it right and who has it wrong—despite the reality that seldom is any one person's identity never-changing and "static."[8] When groups do become static and isolated, they begin to die.

On the one hand, a diaspora can be a place where people who have similar beliefs congregate. A healthy diaspora knows who they are and why they exist. They have clarity about their purpose and what holds them together. The difference between a community that is a healthy diaspora community and one that is not is simple: A healthy one will communicate and interact with groups and communities outside of itself. Healthy diaspora communities invite participation and the crossover of ideas. The sharing of life between those who are part of the diaspora and those who are not is essential in making the community stronger. On the other hand, an unhealthy diaspora community will try to control everything and everyone. It won't be enough to share the common vision and core values and work on common goals; it will seek to control how those are achieved and the tiniest detail of how the community works. An unhealthy diaspora community cuts itself off from the rest of the world and then creates policy for every level of the community, eventually strangling innovation and creativity.

The future Church claims its diaspora quality but also is willing to innovate and take risks. A healthy diaspora can have a place in the world that makes a positive impact on the culture around it, especially if we engage instead of hide, if we use different methods instead of trying to fix the old machines. Hope comes when we take a look at the chaos and see before us not barriers but opportunities. The world around us is a new sea ripe for experimentation and engagement. It is our world. It is our time. It is the world in which we are called to be missionaries. We want to open ourselves up to the themes, events, and technologies already emerging in the world around us. We want to build our capacity to see these as opportunities for creativity and innovation.

## Conjugating Time

If we are going to talk about the future Church, we need to talk about the notion of time. Augustine of Hippo, a great church theologian, wrote in *The Confessions* that when it comes to the construct of time there is no past and no real future. There is only the present. In the present is the memory of the past, so there is what he calls a "present past." In the present is also the idea of the future, so there is the present future.[9] In some way, then, we might say that the present past Church coexists with the present future Church. Embracing our world as a diaspora community means walking with clarity out into the brilliant sunlight of the present future. Bob Johansen and the folks at the Institute for the Future (IFTF) believe that we can see artifacts of the future in our society today.[10] We can see artifacts of our present future Church too. What we do with this information will determine our future.

In 2008, Johansen sat down with leaders of endowed parishes to discuss what the future Episcopal Church might look like. Johansen challenged the group to see the bits and pieces of artifacts from the surrounding culture as "provocative moments." He questioned, "Can we sift through the flotsam and jetsam of the future that even now is washing up upon our shores as we make our way through the perilous waves undaunted?"[11] Today, we are five years into those pregnant ideas having only begun to take our first steps. It seems prudent to look at the material once again and begin to see the reimagined church emerge before us.

If we are going to speak about church communities, we need to look at what is happening in the context around us. If we are going to speak about whom we raise up as missionaries, we look at how people are trained today. If we are to speak about stewardship, we need to look at how people use, spend, and network money. If we are going to talk about service and outreach, then we need to look at how people are doing this today. In each scenario we are able to perceive the gap between where we are today and where the future lies. When we see the gap, we are able then to move into it and begin to create the future Church.

## Church Next

I have, for a number of years, presented a vision for the future of the Episcopal Church:

- The future Church will be driven by the Holy Spirit and cocreated by God's people.
- It will build digital and real commons with a goal of collaboration at every level.
- It will seek unity above all else, even above uniformity.
- It will invest in a life that embraces randomness and creativity, allowing for locally led ministry in a variety of diverse contexts.
- It will become comfortable with interchangeable parts and reusing old traditions in new ways.
- Its organizational structure will change.
- It will change its manner of using authority and engage a ministry of all of God's people.
- It will expect increased participation at every level.
- It will have clear values and be vision-oriented and vision-driven.
- It will be a diaspora but it will not become an island of castaways.
- It will measure different things from the usual standards for success.
- Its leadership will be organic and contextual.
- It will take risks.

The Church today is organized like a locked operating system. In the future, it will allow members to open, rearrange, and play with the product. The contents, therefore, must be easily accessible and the organization must be ready for people to use its resources in various ways.[12]

What does this future Church look like? It will be built upon sound stewardship principles that maintain that all things are God's things—and the question is how are we going to use God's stuff. Communities will build digital platforms and disburse funds in ways that connect the giver with the receiver. This will lead to mission immersion experiences where those who give are also able to do work with their own hands. The church will inspire generosity in giving and in action. It will become entrepreneurial and experimental in its funding of new communities and new congregations. It will understand that the future Church is being formed with technology as a hub of life, not an addition to life. The church's presence in the virtual world will be more important than its address and its phone number.

Clergy and leaders, therefore, will have to rethink how they present who we are and what we do. Clarity about who we are as Episcopalians and how we talk about and experience God through spiritual practice will continue to be elemental in mission. Worship and worship-type experiences beyond Sunday morning and outside of the church will be essential edges for the church. Churches will need to find new forms in which to place our traditions and to use the depth of our tradition as Episcopalians to speak to a whole new generation of people ready to discover and go deep. It will become more and more important for Episcopalians themselves to do this seeking and to draw others closer to an intimate and loving God. This search for deeper spirituality and offering of spiritual experiences will challenge the church to not become a tourist site. The Episcopal Church will have to use its heritage of spiritual depth and ancient tradition and then add to it service to others. The more one interacts with a God of love, the more one will want to serve others. Therefore, the Church will and must remember that these two things are linked both in our tradition and in the desire and hearts of the seekers.

We must know our context well. We must understand the artifacts found in the society around us, and we must seek to engage those artifacts and ask how they are vessels for this mission community. We will need to pattern new rhythms of life and ministry around the ebbs, flows, and movements of the world, always reminding ourselves that our inherited traditions have ancient roots that have been reshaped through the centuries according to time, place, and context. Our context will have its own motion and resistance that needs not so much to be controlled but understood.

Contexts have their own boundaries. Contexts have their own relationships and interrelationships. Contexts interact differently with outside forces, and ours resists certainty and invites wonder.[13] In order for us to move into this new era and navigate it, we will need to become comfortable with a measure of chaos and complexity. "What is being sought," writes biologist Steven Rose, "is a biology that is more holistic and inte-grative, a science that is adult enough to rejoice in complexity."[14] We need to remind ourselves that God is a God of chaos and disorder and is always playing and molding and making. It is true for the church that comes next. It will have to mimic and invite God into cocreative work. Yet not unlike the faithful people of Israel who believed in the Creator God, we may find his hand is already at work in the world around us.

We must be willing to allow ourselves to become accustomed to vola-tility, uncertainty, complexity, and ambiguity. As Nassim Nicholas Taleb writes in his book *Antifragile: Things That Gain from Disorder*, we must allow our "fear to be transformed into prudence, our pain into information, our mistakes into initiation, our desire into undertaking."[15] We must also realize that we are going to have emotions of anger about these changes and that we need to capture and harness that energy into action and invest in good works. As the author of Hebrews writes, "Do not neglect to do good and to share what you have, for such sacrifices are pleasing to God" (Hebrews 13:16).

It is not too late for the Episcopal Church to transform itself into the kind of vessel needed to navigate the waters of the new world of tomorrow. We are a church of tradition and innovation. We are a church of resources spread across seventeen countries. We are a church made up of every kind of human being with every kind of gift with multiple resources. We are a church that has never been afraid of facing difficult tasks or asking hard questions.

God has a mission, and God's mission has the Episcopal Church helping to undertake his reconciling work on earth. Our vision is clear, and it is up to us to bridge the gap between the vision God has of his reign and the reality we experience. It is our work to think intentionally about the shape of the once-imagined and future Church that even now lies before us.

Bob Johansen reminds future leaders that it is up to us to make the future.[16] Leadership, organizational vision alignment, and governance all must shift from being a locked system to an open and usable organism. On the one hand, we must be permission-giving; on the other hand, we must take initiative. The Church exists to invite people to interact with a God who has sought repeatedly to enjoy the diversity of his creation. The good news of salvation, the love of God, and the unique witness of Christ are to be possessed by God's people and not held captive by the Church.

We set our face firmly toward the vision of being a church fully engaged in God's mission. We cannot measure success based on accomplishments or numbers. We will be measured by the transformation that occurred on our pilgrim journey as by the witness of those changed by encountering us along the way. Headway is marked, not with hopelessness about marginalization in an ever secular culture, but with a spirit of joy and excitement about mission work. Not with a fear of failure, but with creativity, experimentation, and a willingness to learn from failure. Despite the diversity of cultural contexts and languages for today's congregations and dioceses, we can focus on serving Christ through evangelism and service to others.

We stand at the precipice of a new age of mission, our own Lemhi Pass. God has called us. We are the ones chosen to remake and rethink strategies for the undertaking of his ministry. Together we take steps into the wilderness as the people of the Episcopal Church, whom Christ calls friends.

## Discussion Questions

1. How would you define the word "shame"? How does shame impact your experience of the church?

2. Bishop Doyle suggests that a healthy diaspora will always communicate and interact with communities and groups outside of itself. What communities does your church currently interact with? How have you seen your church shape these communities? How have these communities shaped your church?

3. Bishop Doyle makes a strong case that innovation is impossible without a strong sense of self-worth. Do you agree? What do you think is the connection between innovation and self-worth?

4. How will the future Church measure its success? Do you believe that measuring success is important for the church? Why or why not?

5. Bishop Doyle lists twelve characteristics of the future Church. What would you remove from his list? What would you add to his list?

## Spiritual Exercise

Bishop Doyle writes, "Healthy diaspora communities invite participation and the crossover of ideas." Think of *one* community within five miles of your church that has different values and a different vision from your faith community. Write down three things you believe that your church could offer that community, as well as three things you think the community could offer your church. If you feel *really* courageous, set up a coffee meeting with someone from the community and share your list.

*Suggested Passage for Lectio Divina:* Luke 5:1–11

## Suggested Reading

Brené Brown, *Daring Greatly: How the Courage to Be Vulnerable Transforms the Way We Live, Love, Parent, and Lead.* New York: Gotham Books, 2012.

Bob Johansen, *The Reciprocity Advantage: A New Way to Partner for Innovation and Growth.* San Francisco: Berrett-Koehler, 2014.

# 4

# Our Guiding Principles

We have, for a while now, been trying to fix things instead of using principled action to guide us. We know who we are, and we know the mission God has given to us. It is also important for us to be clear about our unifying principles: excellence, unity, and connection. These are lived out in the way we undertake our mission.

## Excellence

Our tradition speaks to us about the glory of God. We understand that we are to glorify God. Jesus himself says he comes to glorify God. We are to give to God the best of what we have. We do this through the quality of excellence. We know we won't always get it right, but excellence is something we continually strive toward. We must be honest when we fail, never shaming or shame-filled, and always willing to pick ourselves up and try again. Evangelism, service, stewardship, and formation are marked by excellence when a loving, worshipping community engages God's mission.

## *Excellence in Evangelism*

Excellence in community life is found where Bible study and theological reflection thrive. These activities will change people's lives by sharing the narrative of God in Christ Jesus and helping them learn from him how to live and move and have their being. Excellence in evangelism, though, will not only create followers. Excellence in evangelism will mean developing a community that goes out into the world on the great adventure of apostleship. Jesus never called a disciple (people who follow) that he did not turn into an apostle (people who go) and then send out. He sent out seventy people to preach, heal, and tell people the kingdom of God was at hand.

A community known for its excellence in evangelism will be a community that is intentional about welcoming people into the church. It will be a place that is hospitable and treats every person who enters the house of God as if they were royal guests in God's own house (Luke 7:45ff). At the same time, the future Church will be a church that goes out into the world. The Church must spend more time translating the gospel message across the boundaries we have erected between the Church and the culture. The future Church will spend time finding where God is already at work transforming the lives of real people. We will spend more time working on how to engage our multiethnic, multilingual, and multigenerational culture. We will spend more time crafting a gospel message that is social, cultural, and regional.

The people who became part of the Jesus movement were inspired by the hope that Jesus offered, the transformation of life, and the joy that came from realizing that God loves and embraces his people. The health and strength of the early Christian community was linked to its unity and its diversity. The tremendous growth over the first three centuries happened in a Church with diverse communities and no centralized system of organization. Growth came without a Bible in those first centuries, but instead with the sharing of personal narratives about the healing power of Jesus and the Good News of God's grace. Growth came because of the diversity of community types and the diversity of languages, cultures, and leaders that offered the transformation of the Gospel. This is the witness of Pentecost. Health, strength, and vitality of the Christian community increased because people who loved God and believed in the risen Christ loved their neighbors and served them.

## Excellence in Service

One of the first things the disciples did following the resurrection of Jesus was to increase their number and to ensure that food and care were given to all those in need. They elected deacons specifically to help the community care for and serve those who had no advocates. This, too, is our work. We are to be people who love our neighbor and share what we have. Christian communities living into God's mission will reveal to the world around them excellence in service.

Service is the act of incarnating the gospel of Good News. God's mission of reconciliation and love is revealed in service to our neighbor that transforms lives and restores dignity. The Christian community committed to God's mission can see that the world around them is being changed in concert with Christ's reconciling work. Such communities listen to the needs of the people living in their mission context. They listen and ask what is needed and then invest life, money, time, and creative energy into the problem as a partner with those around them. Excellence in service is what happens when a congregation becomes part of its community and is one of the many who are concerned and act for the betterment of the whole society.

This listening will bring forth initiatives that see neighbors as partners in the work that is needed. Those that are served will have an active role in their own self-care and ministry. Neighbors helping and empowering neighbors is the character of the future Church, not rich people doing something for poor people. If the community around us needs green space, then we will work to create green space. If the community around us says they need help because the schools are in trouble, then we will step in and partner to make the schools a better place. If the community around us believes that the neighborhood is not safe, then we must make sure that everyone knows that the Episcopal Church is a safe place for children and adults. We must be willing to help make our neighborhoods safe instead of building fences, installing alarms, and creating a barricade against the world outside.

Seeing each person as God's beloved is essential to excellent service. Gospel service that has the mark of excellence sees the humanity of others and does not dehumanize them with statistics or stereotypes. Our work is to labor with individuals and see that they and we exist within a complete web of relationships. Service to the whole community is important because we recognize that for people to thrive requires more than the absence of poverty, the absence of infirmity, the absence of hunger.

Excellence in service remembers that Christ himself was always ministering in the midst of widows, children, the oppressed, and the poor. Similarly, the future Church will be part of ministries that help people move from poverty to living wages, from credit-encumbered lives to the freedom to give, from scarcity of food to food security, and from a deficiency of health resources to access to preventive and participatory health education and care. The wellness of a community is dependent upon how well all of this is achieved. In order to accomplish excellence in service, we must do this work and we can't do it alone. We believe we are called to work with others and to share resources, thus reducing our economic footprint while increasing our mission impact. The only way this will happen is by an engagement that includes an honest discussion about money.

## Excellence in Stewardship

We believe in a God that has created a fertile garden in which we can live. We believe in a God who has provided enough food to feed the world, enough natural resources and scientific wisdom to shelter the world. We believe in a God who has provided enough if we will only share by being good stewards of the abundance around us. Using it all up, creating a great divide between the haves and the have-nots, and abusing and exploiting workers for the enrichment of individuals is not good stewardship. The church must engage in God's mission and itself be transformed.

Excellence in stewardship will reveal itself by supporting the vocations of all people. Such stewardship will recognize and employ the many gifts, the wealth of wisdom, and the generosity of God's people and deploy these resources into evangelism and service. We will work to build sustainable mission and ministry for the new age that is not bound by outdated ideas of communication or buildings. Excellence will use the abundant opportunities around the church to increase dollars for mission. Stewardship will move away from concerns about maintenance and self-perpetuation to investment in mission.

## Excellence in Mission

The work before the Church is not a problem to be solved. It is not the kind of thing where we put a group of people in the room and we figure out how to fix everything. Instead, we are an organization built upon faith, and we need to rely upon our faith as we turn outward to engage in the mission field. If we keep coming back to this vision, and if our leaders will allow freedom, we will realize that it is not a disastrous thing to have a variety of new communities and ministries. The future Church is not afraid of people getting out there, pushing the envelope, and doing new things. Visionary leadership will enable us to have the ability to celebrate when we grow and mourn when we fail. Doing this will mean we will be less tempted to ride programs into the ground, spending costly resources and time, when we should shrug it off and move in new directions.

We must let go of the past and stop being enamored of structures—especially structures that mask control instead of freeing up energy for creativity and mission. We, as an organization, have clarity about who we are, and if we will but embrace it and move on, we will be stronger. A fig tree doesn't sit around thinking about what it would do if it were a pecan tree or if it had bark like a pine tree; it is simply a fig tree and it works at being the best fig tree it can be. Deeper, more engaged relationships with the wider community will strengthen our identity and our life, not weaken it. In fact, the idea of a church separate from and outside the life of its community will actually bring about its demise. Churches do not exist as islands unto themselves.

There exists a paradox in living systems: Each organism maintains a clear sense of its individual identity within a larger network of relationships that helps shape its identity. Each organism is noticeable as a separate entity, yet it is simultaneously part of a whole system. In fact, a living organism survives only as it learns how to participate in a web of relationships found in the context in which it makes its home. Churches are always inextricably linked to the community, people, and culture around them. Let us be who we are and reclaim our mission heritage and share Jesus Christ, in the power of the Holy Spirit, in creative ways that enable people of every kind to discover him as savior, and let us join with them and follow him as Lord within the fellowship of his Episcopal Church.

The people who call themselves Episcopalians are people who lead corporate America, who farm the land, who teach in our schools, who work in restaurants and yards, and who live on the street. We are people who fix cars and raise cows and alligators; we are people who sell furniture and run banks. Episcopalians are people who bury the dead, help moms birth the living, and sit with the suffering. We are a giant web of life, of jobs, of ministries and missionary outposts. We are an extensive network of delivery points for the unique story of the Good News of salvation, in word and deed. We as individuals are God's ministers. We are the called. There is no one else. The Holy Spirit rests upon us and we are sent out into the world. This is our time and our moment to act as missionaries of a God who is at work transforming the world. Let us have vision, let nothing interrupt it, and let us undertake our work with urgency. Let us see the future that is all around us and let us act.

Written in 1966 and delivered to his first diocesan council in Texas, Bishop Milton Richardson's words could well be spoken today. Bishop Richardson looked out over a sea of nearly a thousand people at what could easily have been the high-water mark of the Episcopal Church, and he said:

> The World is in ferment today. The Church is in ferment today. Theology is in ferment today. We may mythologize some things surrounding Christ, but we may not mythologize Christ. His Incarnation is a fact. His redemption of us is a fact. The Church as a redeeming body is a fact. And Christ is the great fact—God's fact. And the Trinity is a fact; you cannot say all that you mean by God until you have said Father, Son, and Holy Ghost. The doctrine of the Trinity is as decisively simple and as simply decisive as that.
>
> In an atomic age, the Church with the Holy Scriptures in her hand must proclaim the sovereignty of the power of God as ultimate. In a world of racial prejudice, and national strife, the Church with the historic creeds upon her lips must stand for the unity of the human race in Christ Jesus with no other alternative. In a generation of material wealth, the Church with her sacraments must bear witness to the grace of God as the means of salvation. In a time of great and rapid change and many voices, the Church with her apostolic ministry must speak in no uncertain voice of Him who changeth not and is the Way, the Truth, and the Light.
>
> Two things we need to keep in mind. First, the Lord God reigns. This is His world and He has a purpose for it. Second, we have come into the world at this time to fulfill His purpose.

When the Old Testament Esther hesitated before the danger she faced, Mordecai pointed out her duty, saying, "Who knoweth whether thou art come to the Kingdom for such a time as this?"[1]

I believe that we have been chosen for just such a time as this.

# Unity

Unity over uniformity is an Anglican charism. It is rooted deeply in our history dating back to Queen Elizabeth I, who unified a divided Church during the Reformation. Historical documents like the thirty-nine Articles of Faith that were adopted in the sixteenth century by the Church of England and the nineteenth century by the Episcopal Church speak of the creeds as unifying while worship in every place may be different.[2] Yet there is more to be discovered here. Unity is a basic ingredient for undertaking God's mission and the second of our three guiding principles. The mission will be unsuccessful without unity.

At the core of unity is the very heart of the Gospel—reconciliation. If we do not have clarity about the meaning of reconciliation and how it creates unity among believers, we will forever have difficulty being able to understand how we might be in relationship with those who are different from ourselves. It is this ability to be reconciled with the other that is the only effective seed from which our mission may take root. We should not fool ourselves; how we are in relationship with one another reveals how we are in relationship with God and, in point of fact, reveals how we will treat those who are discovering their own faith.

## Building Bridges

George Barna in his 2003 book *Boiling Point* said that the new millennium would be focused more on our differences than on what we have in common.[3] Community building is a piece of what makes us human. But what makes us human also draws us apart into like-minded groups. Therefore, we are experiencing polarizing extremes. All of us who watch TV, plug into Facebook, or surf the blogosphere know this to be true. We experience a reality where fringe ideas, thoughts, words, and actions come to the front and center of life. In part, this is happening because it is a way to get noticed within the ever greater ocean of information. Bob Johansen of the Institute for the Future warns that "dark innovation" will thrive in this environment.

At the same time, we will also see ideas that would not be viable at any other time in our past take center stage. They will become viable because technology bridges the gap between individuals in such a way that a fringe idea can find followers. Ideas (good and bad) that would have been lost in the sea of time now are gathered into a fringe commons. These ideas now not only make it to the social or real marketplace; they can actually compete in it. New forms of cooperation and platforms for creativity will also become prevalent because of this growing commons. There is a mounting randomness and volatility within the culture, and these polarizing extremes buoy it up.

As a diaspora community that dwells on the edge of culture, this is good but challenging news for the Church. It is good news because we can connect, but we are going to have to be clear about who we are so that we can be found among the thousands of things competing for our attention and loyalty. We will be challenged to build bridges and not engage in polarizing activity ourselves. The new religious age, for example, brings with it individuals who will expect to personalize what they find in our church. We will, on the one hand, be clear about who we are while, on the other, allowing them to personalize their daily spiritual experience.

As we build commons, we will discover we are all intimately connected in one biological system. The Church in this coming age will be challenged to help navigate the bio distress felt within the community. We will need to help during extreme natural disasters, and our responses to hurricanes, fires, and floods will put us on the front lines. We will help individuals find healthy food if they live in food deserts. The Church stepped into the gap in 2014 as unaccompanied children at the U.S. border found themselves in a country that did not want them, reaching out to help during a human disaster of massive proportion.

## *Finding What Unites Us*

It will be very difficult to be a witness for unity and a bridge builder in the culture if we ourselves are divided. In recent years our own church has fallen victim to these cultural disparities. If we are not attentive, they will continue to dismantle our mission—eating us from the inside out as the culture devours us from the outside in.

As a bishop, I often have the pleasure of hearing the blessed Samuel John Stone's hymn "The Church's One Foundation," which was written in 1868. Many believe its theme is connected with the War between the States, but it was, in fact, written for a very different reason. In 1866, an influential and liberal Anglican bishop wrote a book that attacked the historic accuracy of the Pentateuch—the first five books of the Bible, also known as the Torah. Of course, today most Anglicans have come to terms with the idea that the Old Testament is a collection of ancient narratives justifying the kingdom of Israel. But Anglicans also believe that these books contain the Holy Spirit and revelation of who God is in relationship to his people. As you can imagine, at the time this caused a widespread controversy throughout the Anglican Church.

Samuel John Stone, a pastor ministering to the poor of London, was deeply upset by the schism that surrounded him. He wrote a collection of twelve creedal hymns. He understood, above all things, that the foundation of the church must be the Lordship of Christ and not the views of any one group of people. John Stone got it, in my opinion. His hymn "The Church's One Foundation" was based on the Ninth Article of the Apostles' Creed. At the time the words of this section of the creed read: "The Holy Catholic (or Universal) Church; the Communion of Saints; He is the head of this Body." (Yes, we have from time to time changed the words of the creed.) The words of the hymn today always move me and remind me of the awesome work we in the Church choose to undertake, and upon whom we depend most of all. You'll find it in *The Hymnal 1982*; it's number 525. Look it up.

Stone understood that the mission of reconciliation led by Christ was the core and that it united us all as we ministered to the world around us. He understood that without such unity we, our community, and our mission would be lost. We seek to live by these words today despite our common disagreements, our desire to have our own way, our hope for schism, and our sinful want to fight among ourselves.

Throughout his ministry, St. Paul pleaded with the Church to "be in agreement." Let there be "no divisions among you. Be united in the same mind and same purpose," he wrote in his first letter to the Corinthians (1:10). Yet the first Christians were deeply divided over many different things. They were divided because the mission to the Jews and the mission to the Gentiles were in conflict. Much of the Book of Acts and Paul's letters are filled with descriptions of how the early Church dealt with what was essentially a conflict created by two colliding cultures. Rather than appealing to the law, Paul reminded believers of the freedom they have in

Christ. Christians, Paul insisted, are free to follow their conscience and are free from the burden of judging or changing others. Christians are prohibited from indicting and sentencing those who are different because of the freedom we have in Christ Jesus.[4]

How can a Church divided still "be in agreement"? The first Christians embraced the gospel truth that Christ is our unity. What glues the Church together is "the message of the cross," Paul wrote (1 Cor. 1:18). Our diverse yet faithfully held positions shall in the end be laid at the altar of God. Until that time, our faith in Jesus Christ unites us and draws us into the mission field. In this we find a manner of living with one another in a covenant community. If we imitate Christ and his manner, we too will find unity in our faith and in our work. Paul's words challenge us to be unified for mission some two thousand years later.

## Overcoming What Divides Us

In our conflicts we spend so much time attempting the destruction of one another that there is nothing left in the relationship. By our very nature, we find it enticing to have an enemy we can consume rather than a brother or sister whom God invites us to make family. The gospel challenges us, through the blessings of a grace received, to empty ourselves of our desires to judge and condemn so that we may befriend our fellow Christian with the love, mercy, and forgiveness of Jesus for the purpose of reconciliation and service. This is the unifying mind of Christ. It is a unity that understands hospitality and love and is obedient no matter how abusive someone else might get. You and I are challenged by the reconciling love of Jesus Christ to be different from the world around us. Jesus took up his cross, and we are to do the same.

After meeting all day, a few bishops gathered late one evening to talk and solve the problems of the world. One bishop got really angry and said the "other side" deserves what they get because they were so hostile to the minority long ago. I challenged him (and myself). I said that the task of the Christian is not to require an eye for an eye, but to be a witness of grace and mercy no matter what is given. A Christian will let go of the natural desire to harm in order to have the mind of Christ, which is to love. When ideological opponents in the church can cease judgment of one another and serve one another, only then is the mission of Christ successful. When we have the mind of Christ and act with mercy, grace, love, and kindness, then the kingdom of God is revealed before us.

God is our unity. This is the truth that Scripture reveals and that Paul and Peter tried to convey to the earliest Church. When someone leaves and chooses to live outside of the community, they move away from God. God is building communities of diverse people who don't all agree; that is the way he made us. The rector for whom I first worked once looked me in the eye and said to me, "Andy, God will not bless division and conflict. It is not God's way." I think he is marvelously correct. When we turn inward and fight among ourselves, God does not bless our efforts, and the fruits of our labor rot upon the tree. God does not bless our division, because I don't believe that God is present in these battles. When we fight one another we are about as far away from the truth of God's reconciling ministry as one can possibly be.

As Episcopalians and Anglicans, some elements of our common life are more important than others. Theologically, I rank the hierarchy of elements of conformity in this way. I would place sharing the Good News of salvation and the uniqueness of Christ (Matt. 28:18ff), which we call evangelism, alongside Christ's command to love our neighbor and be an aid and comfort to the poor, those in prison, the young and the old, which we call service to others (Matt. 25), as the key unifying elements upon which the missionary church stands. In other words, God has a mission of reconciliation, and the key unifying nature of the church is to be found in our undertaking together the work of that mission.

Then come the secondary unifying principles for Anglicans, which help us gather ideas and concepts around these first principles: the Scriptures, creeds, historic councils, the threefold order of ministry, and prayer book worship. Entwined and linked to every one of these elements are the two sacraments of the Anglican Church: baptism and the Eucharist. They impart "grace unearned and undeserved."[5] They are the two sacraments of the gospel given by Christ to his Church.

At yet a lower level are the other "sacramental rites evolved in the church under the guidance of the Holy Spirit." The prayer book catechism goes on to say that while they are a means of grace in our tradition, marriage and the other sacramental rites "are not necessary for all persons in the same way that Baptism and Eucharist are."[6] The things we spend our time on are the things of less importance. We might then consider the topic of marriage in its appropriate sacramental space within the life of the church locally and the communion globally. Is it important? Yes. Is the money, time, membership, and energy lost in the conflict over marriage serving the proclamation of the gospel? I think not.

We must honor the fact that, in reality, we do not all agree. We are not unified and there are emotions and personal investment in our opinions. As one blogger posted, "I am ok as long as I don't have to change my principles." Unity as an effective instrument for mission is more than simply reordering our thinking and living with toleration for our neighbor and our neighbor's ideas.

## Reconciled—with God and Each Other

Many people today are speaking about the work of reconciliation as a Christian value that speaks to this notion of unity. My own diocese has chosen the word reconciliation as a value, stating: "We are reconciled to Christ and to one another." Archbishop of Canterbury Justin Welby has made reconciliation one of his three goals.

The mission of reconciliation is the heart of the Christian gospel. Reconciliation has both a vertical dimension and a horizontal one. The vertical dimension speaks to God's relationship with humanity through the death and resurrection of Jesus Christ. I believe this applies to all people, not just some. It also applies to the "world" in general. This is the Good News meant for all people. This is why Jesus is the friend of sinners. There is plenteous forgiveness, and we are all reconciled to God—there is no scarcity in the gospel. The horizontal dimension of reconciliation speaks to humanity's relationship with our neighbor. All have been reconciled to each other through the death and resurrection of Jesus Christ (past tense). In God's eyes, our reconciliation with one another is an accomplished fact.

The vertical dimension of reconciliation precedes the horizontal dimension. In other words, God's reconciliation with humanity and the individual creates and necessitates the individual's reconciliation with his or her neighbor. Both the vertical dimension and the horizontal dimension of reconciliation are the work of God. It is God's faithful reconciliation work that is revealed in us as we are faithful. Thus, the Church's work is to "wake up" to the truth that we have been reconciled and to live in accordance with this truth "so that the world might know" God's reconciliation, too. Our eyes are to be wide open. Thus, to borrow Alexander Schmemann's phrase, the Church lives as a reconciled people "for the life of the world."[7] As Paul says, God is making his appeal to the world through us (2 Cor. 5:20).

The implication is that when we say things like "reconciliation is the work of the Church" what we really mean is "waking up to the theological truth that God has already reconciled us to one another and the world to himself" is the work of the church. We don't create reconciliation. We wake up to and increasingly embrace reconciliation. Reconciliation with one another is not something we need. What we need is to stop all of our self-righteous, stubborn, and illusion-based behaviors that keep us blind to the truth that already we are one.

In the recognition that God is the reconciling agent in our midst, we all come closer to God and to one another. Furthermore, the witness of such a reconciled community draws into itself the beautiful and wonderful diverse people of God. The Church to come will be a church at ease with itself. The future Church will be a church unified and one that works across boundaries of confessional exactitude.

# Connection

The future Church is connected. Throughout the Gospels, it is revealed that Jesus loved his followers as friends and that he intended that they in turn love the world as friends. In John 15, Jesus teaches his followers about his relationship with God and what that meant for his relationships with his followers. Jesus tells them that he is intimately connected with God. He gives them an image of a vine with branches that is bearing fruit. He says, in effect, "Being in relationship with God is about being connected. When we are all connected to one another and to God we change the world—we bear fruit. Fruit doesn't just happen—it comes from being connected to God, just like fruit and a vine." Jesus tells them that those who follow him are to be connected and that this connection and their work to love each other will change lives. "Joy comes from being loved and loving others, joy comes from being connected to God, to others, and to me," Jesus says. So Jesus tells them: "This is my commandment, that you love one another as I have loved you."

## Affection Is Connection

Jesus tells them that they are his friends. He reminds them economies of the world work in a lot of different ways. In the world of Jesus's day there are servants and there are masters. This is true for our day as well. He tells his followers that their worth and their value in the world around them is always and everywhere going to be based upon what they can do, how they can serve, and what they can trade. He then makes it clear that this is not the way God works. God loves. God loves them. Jesus loves them. They are his friends and he needs nothing from them—they are not servants and he is not the master. In John's Gospel, more than any other, Jesus and his followers are bound together by the commandment of loving each other. Their affection will show the world that they are connected to Jesus and through Jesus to God. Affection was the binding tie.

A recent Pew Research poll on the politicization of America finds that not only are like-minded people likely to live in the same places and like the same things, they are also more likely to hang out with friends who believe similar things.[8] This means that friendship can easily lead to isolating communities. But the mission of the gospel is for everyone, and the Christian community is open to everyone. "Affection is connection," wrote poet and author Wendell Berry.[9] Affection is the quality of relationship that Jesus speaks about and the quality of relationships that people are seeking as they yearn in the midst of a disjointed and disconnected world.

### Thinking Small

I have learned from the maker movement that it takes the same amount of energy and time to make a custom item as it does to mass-produce it. We are seeing a rise in personal fabrication that then is marketed and connected to friends and neighbors. Scale is no longer the quintessential goal of business. More and more people are baking, distilling, and creating businesses in their homes and selling to their friends. What is coming into view is a society that is restructuring itself organically. Children are writing computer programs, creating art, building their own networks. Adults are crafting things in their garages. Technology and communication tools are shifting monthly. New micro-economy and secondary markets are growing. New currencies and new forms of connecting with investors are changing start-ups with crowd-sourced technology. People are relating and cocreating at a colossal level.

Gorbis comments on this, saying, "The future lies in micro-contributions by large networks of people creating value on a scale previously unthinkable, bringing sociality and social connectivity back into our economic transactions, in the process redefining notions of rewards, incentives, growth, and currencies." This will affect how our Christian communities work and how they build relationships. This means that Christian communities, thanks to technology and the maker movement, can exist on small budgets with few staff and still reach large numbers of people through their ministry.[10] The hallmark of the Christian community of the future is that they will connect people—and connect people to God.

## Sharing Resources

The living Church will be a church of affection, because connection is what makes all the other pieces work together. The shape of our communities will also depend upon a network of very real relationships. This network is apparent when we look at the rise in congregations starting new communities. Connections take on a physical nature as congregations create their own web. The younger generations of believers and seekers are interested in very real connection and relationships as they navigate their world. Younger clergy have a great interest in this mission field. Nadia Bolz-Weber, founder of House for All Sinners and Saints, a Lutheran congregation in Denver, does not have an office but has office hours all over the city, shares worship space with another church, and does service ministry in collaboration with other nonprofit organizations. She and her community are plugged into the world around them—networking, sharing, and multiplying.

I have been talking about this since I began teaching about generations in the 1990s. We've seen a surge in networks of connected churches sharing resources. These are churches starting second sites and planting new communities.[11] You might think of these as small-batch Christian communities. Nondenominational churches, which are freed from structural concerns, are leading the way in many respects. A few Episcopal churches in our own diocese are beginning to think this way; today we have eight second-site communities in the Diocese of Texas. A church networking into another part of the broader community began each site. I expect that while some will continue to multiply, and others will not be successful, this will be a growing trend across the future Church. The cost of staff and facilities, the lack of available large spaces, and a desire of people not to travel far for church recommend this approach.

A report on multisite congregations released by the Leadership Network in 2013 shows that while they are often small, they are growing as much as 14 percent per site per year. Because of the size and the personality of these communities, more people participate in leadership.

Multisite communities depend on lay leadership more than clergy. Multisite communities are found in urban, suburban, and rural settings.[12]

A number of multisite congregations are created when one church combines with another. We saw this in Houston when St. Luke's Methodist took on the Gethsemane Methodist campus, which was formerly a stand-alone parish. Now St. Luke's shares resources and runs ministry and service projects out of the Gethsemane campus. They have multiplied their connections and networks across the city, into areas St. Luke's never would have reached alone. Large congregations have been the "pioneers," but today congregations as small as fifty are experimenting with the multisite model.

## Building Networks

Everyone born in the new millennium will be a *digital native*. This will be true for the rich and the poor alike. I was struck when I visited Southern Malawi in 2009 and saw that everyone had a cell phone. They might not have had running water or indoor plumbing but they had a cell phone. Recently, a doctor at one of the finest medical schools in the country, speaking about telemedicine and accessibility, talked to me about visiting the poorest widow in East Africa in a hut where she had a stool and little else—but she had a cell phone. We are moving into an era of unparalleled accessibility and connectivity. If you are not a digital native, if you didn't grow up in the digital age, then you are called a *digital migrant*.

Over the last decade I have watched as the Church encountered the new digital age. Man, it is slow! Getting congregations to understand how important connections through electronic media are for people has been, as we say in Texas, "like pushing string up a hill." Today the majority of churches and church leaders do not use social media at all, despite the fact that 74 percent of the mission field does this as a normal part of everyday life.

Over the next twenty years we are going to see the birth of an entirely new Internet that, as it evolves, will connect humans in new ways. We as human beings are adapting and adopting technology to fit our demanding lives and our desire for connection in real time with a global population. Just look at the way the Internet has developed. It was created to store information. Then it became a way of passing information from one source to another. It further developed to a web, where information could be pushed and people could stake out space.

In the last five years we have shifted our focus in the Diocese of Texas to push information throughout our networks. However, in the future we will be changing our strategies again as the networking possibilities are multiplied. Yesterday the computer was the center of the experience. I had to learn how to use it, and I could use it only on its terms. Today humans are the center of the experience.[13] Computers work more intuitively based upon how we think and how we work. We are mobile and the technology we are using is mobile and responsive to our needs.

The environment in which we do ministry is no longer an environment located purely in the physical world, but within an environment of space. Think for a moment about the fact that when I was a child I grew up learning to write and then to type. When I typed I had to leave two spaces after a sentence. Now the computer automatically creates the right amount of space between sentences and even corrects my spelling. Today a child knows how to use a touch screen before she knows how to spell her own name.[14]

In order to reach the digital natives of the future, communicate with them, and engage them, the church must migrate into their digital world. We are moving away from the idea that priests make house calls and people come to a church building for spiritual direction. In the future a successful priest's ministry will rely upon being able to keep up with the congregation electronically—all the time, all week long. Priests will have to use all the tools at their disposal, from text messaging to online engagement on Twitter, Facebook, Instagram, video chatting, or whatever comes along next. While the medical profession is moving to telemedicine, the Church remains firmly rooted in mid-century evangelism and pastoral care models.

## The Rewards of Participation

The Church has been focused on an old network economy, where the Church pays individuals to be professional ministers and to network the congregation. This era is over. The future Church will thrive on nonmonetary rewards for service and ministry. People will contribute their time, effort, and money because they experience community when they participate. They gain in their relationships. They gain by "belonging." They also will do the work on their own time in their own imperfect way. This is more authentic.

The rest of the culture has become accustomed to homemade video and communications that are real and not staged. The church will have to become accustomed to letting down its guard a bit in order to engage what is available to it. We as a Church have forgotten that the Church in the end is not a business but a web of connections. The reward of participation in Church life, in Christian community, has always been a reward far beyond what we receive by attending worship. These nonmonetary rewards remind us that if we as Christian communities truly invest in work that is transformative, we will have an army of communicators helping us to get the word out about the good things that God is doing.

The connected Church will understand that these kinds of rewards work best at the grassroots level. The Church is deeply rooted in an industrial model from the last century, when the big company was king and the Church mimicked it. Larger-than-life preachers with larger-than-life churches have been a goal, and big churches with big ministries have served as foundation stones in many dioceses. Some believe these will go away, but I don't think so. I think they will remain as long as, and especially if, they are willing to support new communities and ministries in the world. If they don't, they will have difficulty navigating the future. Strong networks of many individuals will outperform and out-transform larger churches, and have a smaller price tag too.

We see a growing number of small Christian communities, but it is sometimes said that because they are not large, they are not successful. It is old thinking that the church is only successful if it has a lot of people. They *are* successful in meeting individuals where they are and engaging with their own mission field, where individual transformation and the transformation of the local community are prized over size.

The connected Church of the future will be a church that uses its network of individuals to build new social commons. The connected Church will enable and raise up visionaries to see new mission opportunities for evangelism, for service, and for stewardship. The connected Church will organically raise up digital commons and then plant real-life communities. New platforms will be developed to help the connected disciples work together to make people's lives better.

What we see today in the economic world is that a person is no longer a designer, or an engineer, or a production line worker, or a shopper. Instead one person can be all of these things and be their own company too. And with the invention of apps like Square, which allows people to use a credit card to transfer money from one individual to another, commerce can take place anywhere and at anytime.[15] The future Church will be mobile. It can take shape anywhere, at anytime, and with any number of people, without the structures of the present church to inhibit its growth. Suffice it to say that the future looks more like the first-century Church than the Protestant professionalism of the last century.

## The Ministry of All

For the future Church, there will be many questions about embracing the ministry of all the baptized and the use of the various orders of ministry. Instead of a church community organized around people with funny collars, how will we capitalize on the maker culture? People want to contribute and participate in shaping the life of their church. The Episcopal Church and other mainline denominations will be challenged to move away from the idea that the "people" are those who get ministered *to* by the "professional sacramentalist." Instead, we must begin to think about capturing the new desire and energy to be involved (not as a volunteer) as a leader and cocreator. No longer is the Church to be led by clergy and supported by people. The future Church will be supported by clergy and led by the people.

The denominational church still operates predominately with one building and one priest. We now have an opportunity to see that lightweight structures, networked communities, and new methods of organization offer a whole new model of commons making. In the 1980s, we used to say that the big churches were getting bigger and the small churches were getting smaller and were going to close. Quite simply put, we were as a whole uninterested in a church that had fewer than 150 people, unless we believed it would grow. Today we need to learn from the small church *and* the big church. We need to imagine cooperative commons-making for small churches and big churches. The VUCA world is an equal-opportunity change agent. Now is the time to embrace new models.[51]

# Discussion Questions

1. Bishop Doyle begins this chapter by asserting, "We have been trying to fix things instead of using principled action to guide us." What do you think he means by this? Do you agree? How does a church gain clarity about its unifying principles?

2. What deeply held principles guide your life when you are at your best? When did these principles emerge as being important to you? When do you find it most difficult to live by your principles?

3. What is the difference between excellence and perfectionism? Can a church strive for excellence without slipping into perfectionism?
4. Bishop Doyle says that "unity over uniformity is an Anglican charism." Do you agree? What do you see as the basis of our unity as Episcopalians? As Christians?
5. List all the ways in which the future Church will be more connected than it is now. What excites you about this list? What scares you about this list? What new behaviors do you need to learn to connect with the church and the world in a more meaningful way?

## Spiritual Exercise

Prayerfully read 1 Corinthians 12 out loud. After several moments of contemplative silence, reread the passage a second time and answer the following questions: How does St. Paul define unity? What is the relationship between unity and difference? As a result of this meditation, write down *one thing* you believe that God invites you to do differently to help cocreate the future Church. Take action based on your answer.

*Suggested Passage for Lectio Divina:* Philippians 2:4–11

## Suggested Reading

Peter L. Steinke, *Congregational Leadership in Anxious Times: Being Calm and Courageous No Matter What.* Herndon, VA: Alban Institute, 2006.

Peter Scazzero, *Emotionally Healthy Spirituality: It's Impossible to Be Spiritually Mature, While Remaining Emotionally Immature.* Grand Rapids, MI: Zondervan, 2014.

# 5

# Autopoietic Communities

Niels Bohr and Werner Heisenberg were physicists. They had a problem. They were trying to understand the universe, but every time they would pursue a question in an experiment, the universe proposed something that, despite sound reasoning from acceptable premises, led to conclusions that were logically unacceptable and/or self-contradictory.[1] Their discourses were, of course, the beginning of quantum theory. Margaret Wheatley points out in her book *Leadership and the New Science: Discovering Order in a Chaotic World*, "Their problem was not only intellectual but involved an intense emotional and existential experience."[2]

The world they knew, the rules of order they functioned under, and the world they were recording at the microscopic level were completely different. Heisenberg spoke of it this way: "Can nature possibly be so absurd as it seemed to us in these atomic experiments?"[3] "Every experiment," he reflected, "destroys some of the knowledge of the system which was obtained by previous experiments."[4]

What Heisenberg and Bohr's experience has taught me is that the world is filled with explanations for why things are the way they are, and those explanations often contradict one another. The world is complex beyond our imagination.[5] The world's complexity fools us into seeing linear reactions that are only a small portion of the reality swirling around us. They may not even be linear. Daniel Kahneman writes: "Our comforting conviction that the world makes sense rests on a secure foundation: our almost unlimited ability to ignore our ignorance."[6] It can take individuals who lead organizations a long time to step back, accept the paradoxes and contradictions of their findings, and then begin to reframe the questions.

Acceptance is never without some amount of pain. Margaret Wheatley reflects on the process the physicists experienced: "Its effect on physicists' view of reality was truly shattering. The new physics necessitated profound changes in concepts of space, time, matter, object, and cause and effect; and because these concepts are so fundamental to our way of experiencing the world, their transformation came as a great shock. The story speaks with a chilling familiarity. Each of us recognizes the feelings this tale describes, of being mired in the habit of solutions that once worked yet that are now totally inappropriate, of having rug after rug pulled from beneath us."[7] Wheatley adeptly applies this revelation to organizations. It is time that we apply them to the organization we call the Church.

For example, I grew up in church ministry believing that everything was magically connected to the Average Sunday Attendance (ASA) of my congregation. What had happened is that in the early eighties the idea of congregational development became an important concept for those who deeply wanted to change the downward trend in church. Before this time, diocesan leadership had pretty much treated every priest and every congregation the same. Books and theories began to circulate about congregations and church size that provided some helpful insights. However, the church began to make our ASA *the* most important measurement tool for health and vitality. Everything got focused on raising your attendance. After thirty years of this focus within our church, the ASA number is still the most sacred sign of supposed health for the church. Leaders base our feelings of success and our feelings of failure upon that number.

But a church's ASA is poor indication of its health. I first became aware of this when I was reading Bill Bryson's book *At Home: A Short History of Private Life.* It is about a house that he purchased in England, an old vicarage. The house had been built for the local Anglican priest sometime around 1851. Bryson becomes interested in a statistic he discovers in his research about the home. In 1851 the Church of England decided to find out how many of its folks attended church, so it surveyed all its churches. What they discovered was that only 20 percent of the people went to church.[8] What an odd thing, I thought. Then I realized I had been *assuming* that somehow, before I came along, everyone had just gone to church every Sunday. Now if you stop and think about it for a moment you would realize that, of course, not everyone went to church. I would have guessed 90 percent of the people in England went to church in 1851. In my mind, I had always thought that there were churches full of people. And, it was just my unhappy luck that I was born and called into ministry in a time when very few people went to church.

This little bit of information really blew my mind. In my struggle to grasp this new reality, I became painfully aware that my basic concepts, language, and whole way of thinking about community life were inadequate to describe the context I now inhabited. That was it. I had inherited a wonderful idea of church. Church was the place where every Sunday Mom and Dad took little Andy, along with all the other neighbors and their children. I began to realize that it was perhaps true that Sunday morning attendance in the 1950s and 1960s had been the high-water mark of Protestant church attendance in the United States. But by no means was it normative to the Christian experience. I realized that I had a lot of shame about the ASA numbers in my church as a young priest. I didn't feel good enough since my numbers didn't match the magical church ideal of the ever-growing church with its ever growing ASA. I also realized there was a whole lot more to the reality of Christian community than a church and its ASA number.

While I do believe that the average Sunday attendance numbers of any given congregation can actually predict a particular economic formula for a particular type of church, I have decided that a focus on ASA can be detrimental to the health of the Church at large. In reading Margaret Wheatley's book, I realized that the way we use averages themselves do funny things and can play tricks on our ability to understand cause and effect. Big numbers are easy to manipulate and get our minds around. However, when we look at the big numbers, we may miss micro information that is essential in understanding community and cultural dynamics. Wheatley believes that in the "small fluctuations" of life and relationships there is a lot of "ambiguity and complexity" that affects the world in which we move and have our being.[9] If you are a large organization, you really don't have time for such detail. Dioceses have to use averages and large frameworks to avoid the complexity of congregational life and context, because such large entities don't have enough staff to deal with the diversity. Wheatley argues that large organizations actually "shield" themselves from the details that are life-giving.[10] The problem is that growth, energy, and innovation come out of the micro connections oftentimes hidden within the complexity of the system. In point of fact, the very health of the whole organization rests upon the health and vitality of the smallest relationships. It is out of these micro relationships that creativity and innovation spring, giving life to the whole.

Nassim Nicholas Taleb, in his book *Black Swan*, amplifies theories regarding the reality that randomness and variability are very real participants in making history. He says, "History is opaque. You see what comes out, not the script that produces events. . . . The generator of historical events is different from the events themselves, much as the minds of the gods cannot be read just by witnessing their deeds."[11] He also explains the reality that we have difficulty not categorizing everything. He says, "Because our minds need to reduce information, we are more likely to try to squeeze a phenomenon into the Procrustean bed[12] of a crisp and known category (amputating the unknown), rather than suspend categorization, and make it tangible. Thanks to our detections of false patterns, along with real ones, what is random will appear less random and more certain—our overactive brains are more likely to impose the wrong, simplistic, narrative than no narrative at all."[13] Clear as mud? Did he just use Procrustean bed in a sentence? That is a Brobdingnagian concept, Taleb! Take a moment to read it again, and remember it; we'll return to our own Procrustean bed later.

Kahneman agrees with Taleb, and I am afraid, adds even more suspicion to the way in which we tell our stories about history. He writes, "The confidence that individuals have in their beliefs depends mostly on the quality of the story they can tell about what they see, even if they see little." This is a principle he calls WYSIATI: What You See Is All There Is. Kahneman says that the systematic part of our brains is lazy and so we typically jump to conclusions based upon intuitive impressions rather than difficult thinking.[14]

All this reading made me rethink how I had ordered my intuition about Church history. Church history is taught in a linear fashion, and because you can only see what you are taught (and WYSIATI) it is no wonder that we have developed an over-simplified understanding of our church, its origins, and its perfect trajectory to this moment in time. This is called a *hindsight bias*. Kahneman writes: "The mind that makes up narratives about the past is a sense-making organ. . . . A general limitation of the human mind is its imperfect ability to reconstruct past states of knowledge, or beliefs that have changed."[15] If we are going to ponder what the future may look like, we have to come to terms with the fact that the past probably was not much like what our intuitive biases tell us it was like.

Let us look again, as if for the first time, at the formation of church. The earliest texts seem to reveal that the first followers of Jesus were people who lived in a variety of communities: they lived in urban and rural areas; many were Jews but plenty of others were not. This intermingling of people from diverse social levels, each living out their faith, created an environment of energized innovation and creativity. This is certainly the vision of the early followers that is recorded and remarked upon in the Gospels, the Book of Acts, and the Epistles. I think we can also say that the Jesus movement was, in its earlier days, a kind of subculture within the culture, and went unnoticed for quite a while. It was not like Jesus was resurrected, the Holy Spirit came down, and boom there were churches.

The letters of Paul to the different communities offer an early and clear record that one of the ways individuals got together was in their own homes. Paul is continually remarking on so-and-so's "house." While Paul's letters are often addressed to a church, each city's church had a number of small house churches. In Paul's letter to Philemon, it is clear that Philemon's house church was one of many in the city of Colossa. We should, however, dismiss any theory that says that there were only house churches or there were only urban churches. We see clearly in the literature that both coexisted, along with societies such as clubs, guilds, colleague groups, and burial societies.[16]

While the Pauline churches appear to have been more unified in terms of social rank, the societies were more open to a cross-section of society because they were based less on family or social connections, and more on the criteria of belonging. These societies coexisted as self-contained and unique organizations—they were located to their context.

There was, in fact, still another type of community that was randomly being generated during the same period of time. Many of the first followers of Jesus were Jews, so they founded communities within synagogues. Many of these groups would soon be identified as Christians and kicked out of the synagogues. So the nature and liturgy of synagogue worship was very important to this community. Throughout the Mediterranean region unused or abandoned synagogues would be reinhabited or taken over by Christians. Some of the first buildings we might call churches began their lives as synagogues. The ones we know of from Paul's letters and archeological digs are Duro Europos, Stobi, and Delos.

Schools were still another kind of Christian community. Similar to philosophical schools of the day, this is where followers of Jesus would gather around a teacher. These learning groups, which could include professionals and students, met together, learned together, and debated one another. They grew and some would become communities in and of themselves.

While the cities appeared to be swelling with a variety of communities, so too were rural areas. Out of the desert came a more communal expression of early Christianity. Communities of cave-dwelling desert fathers, small groups of praying women, and communes separated themselves from society to prepare for Jesus's return. These movements can easily be seen as the seeds of the monastic movements to come.

During the time when the Church was growing faster than it ever has, we can see that there were many different kinds of groups of Christians gathering together. I have mentioned the ones we know about. But this can't possibly be a complete inventory of the Christian communities that existed. Remember, WYSIATI. These are only the ones we have read about or dug up. There were, in fact, many forms and ways of participating. People believed different things and people worshipped in different ways. People gathered at different times of the week in different places. So what happened?

In this diverse and growing period of our communal life, the focus was on relationships. It was the relationship with the risen Lord and their relationships with one another that mattered most. Space, liturgy, vessels, roles, theologies, unanimity, and ways of being community were varied and were not the communities' primary concerns. Archeological evidence reveals that commonplace objects, common places, and common meals were the focus of the relational act of gathering.

As the communities (that we know about) grew and organized, more emphasis moved to the defining roles of place and liturgy. By CE 300 we have unified and common liturgies, a developing customary, and vessels that are made specifically for liturgical use.[17] The spaces begin to be organized around the gathering of the people as opposed to being a space that just happened to be where people found themselves. The importance of space and content would continue to evolve.

By the eighth century, the ordinary has become the special. The ordinary household materials gathered and used for the breaking of common bread in whatever place the faithful gathered are now transformed. The pottery cup and plate taken from the cupboard now are gold and silver formed for the special purpose of celebrating the Lord's Supper. Along with the special vessels comes the standardization of the service itself.[18] Special buildings set apart from the common home become community centers for the life of the faithful. Abbeys for those who follow the strictest of rules have formed. Shrines dot the Holy Land. People make pilgrimages to see the sacred sites, reenacting moments of Christ's life. There seems to be a never ending growth in hierarchy, the setting aside of places of worship, and the formalization of worship. Even what were normal street clothes in the first century are now beautiful vestments signifying roles in the eucharistic feast.

By 1517, the high-water mark of the universal faith that is Christianity, buildings and liturgy are no longer about the people but about the action. What is happening is mysterious and not very earthly, and a high priesthood is in charge of the holy items.[19] The holy world is wholly separate from the real world, and the heavenly banquet table is to be carefully and ritually prepared by the professional.

Now we have arrived at the Reformation, the great divide that is also a great moment of reinvention of the church. The culture focused upon the nature of knowing—epistemology. In the Church, the great movements of the Reformation were about the Bible, liturgy, and language. There was a rediscovery of a living theology, broadcast in the language of the people. Homes and churches were filled with a new vibrancy of faith. This of course cannot be understated. The reform would spread and Christianity would continue to grow, but it grew within the vessel that had become the norm—a church building. The church is the building where the people go for the sacraments (Roman) or to hear the living word preached (reformed). What happens during the succeeding three hundred years is a bumpy road but mostly unchanged until the invention of free time.

While some will want to focus on the monastic reformations, or the discoveries of ancient manuscripts, or liturgical revivals, I want to focus on the creation of free time. The Victorians are responsible for this invention. No matter what we look at—the creation of public parks, the shortening of the work week, the increase in what people called pastime, or the growing understanding of something called "childhood"— all came into fashion during the late nineteenth century.[20] For the first time, people began to think about time that was *not* spent working. Prior to this time, most people worked all the time. It was *survival* that set the hours of the day. They would only from time to time make their way to the local shrine for a holy feast day. What began to happen next will tell the tale for a hundred years: the church began to grow in attendance. Not only did the Victorians invent pastime, they decided to spend it going to church. The minister and preaching were some of the best entertainment there was to be had.

In the United States, the expansion of cities, growth in population in the West, and the unchallenged sacred time of Wednesday nights and Sunday mornings saw the great expansion in church attendance. By the end of this boom in the 1950s, the diocese I serve had planted five congregations a year for a decade, almost doubling what it had during the previous hundred years. The Diocese of Texas was not alone in this expansion. The Church began to build monolithic bureaucracies and hierarchies. Our presiding bishop appeared on the cover of *Time* magazine. Money rich, we sent out missionaries, and our church itself began to expand into new countries.

We also turned inward. New scholarship allowed for a reinvention of liturgy. By the twentieth century the liturgical movement had returned the central action of the Eucharist to weekly worship. The liturgical renewal movement also brought with it a new liturgical fundamentalism as we became overly focused on the words we say, the words the priest says, and the words of the Bible. Fundamentalism sneaked in and Christians began to argue over inerrancy. Politics crept in and we began to argue about culture issues. Words and their meaning became important and we argued over the gender of God, sexuality, the gender of ministers, the place of divorced people. We argued and we argued. Along with the rest of the Western culture, we divided ourselves into camps at war with one another. We began to break apart our churches as if playing out C. S. Lewis's *The Screwtape Letters*. In it a senior devil instructs his emissary to keep the Christians fighting among themselves. Paul has similar warnings about division. Yet, we become the arbiters of truth, and the great dismantling of Western Christianity begins.

I am not judging this part of our history, though it would have been nice if someone had been paying attention to the dramatic changes taking place. I think you can see only what you can see. The church and her leadership did not see what was coming. Here is the important thing: because we did not do evangelism and discipleship, but waited for people to come through our doors, today we are in trouble and out of shape.

At the same moment that we were busy, there was a seismic shift in the culture. Philosopher Charles Taylor, in his book *A Secular Age*, called it a "mass phenomenon."[21] The culture, Taylor offers, is caught in an immanent frame. The mechanical world jettisoned a "hierarchy of being" and there was an "atrophy of a sense of God."[22] The transcendent world was rejected for a natural world without mystery. Everything could be explained in reference to itself. There was no need for the individual life to be dependent upon or in relationship with God. Instead, the "buffered human being" was self-sufficient.[23] Even society was able to reveal its own "blueprint" for how things are to "hang together" for the "mutual benefit" of the whole.[24] In the end there would be no need for God or religion. The Church was, all in all, unprepared to speak a living word into this culture shift. In fact, the Church willingly adapted to it and settled into a diaspora relationship with the culture. Harvey Cox wrote in his musing on the secular city, "The failure of modern theology is that it continues to supply plausible answers to questions that fewer and fewer people are asking."[25] Not unlike those in the twentieth century, we continue to answer questions and problems from a period that no longer exists.

These shifts in thinking were accompanied by a shift in technology. By the 1960s, all institutions felt the effects of a rapidly evolving culture. Technology introduced itself to people. TV and other media took up residence in the living room. Sacred weeknights were given to sports and after-school activities. Sacred Sundays were taken up by more sports and family activities. Did I mention there was more TV to watch? New media and communications provided spiritual information in the privacy of your own home. The end of a great cataclysmic shift has dissolved the church's place at the center of the entertainment, communication, spirituality, family, and neighborhood life. So the church shrank, and financial burdens grew, and the culture changed. All put the nails in the coffin of the past model of doing church.

What we did next was to try and fix the problem. We thought if we just were more welcoming, or more attractive, or bigger and had more programs, we would be okay. We spent time on words, music, and liturgy. We thought that relevance was where we should put our energies, so we tried to be relevant, which came off a little gimmicky. We thought if we could understand the nature of each generation we could better market the church. What became clear is that we didn't have enough consultants. We knew that if we just had more consultants we would be golden. We bought a lot of books to help us better understand the nature of communities. We spent a lot of time organizing things. It is like arranging deck chairs on the Titanic. In the do-better mode we thought we could categorize our churches.

Our Procrustean bed was the categorization of church by size.

In the 1980s, a truly brilliant man, Arlin Rothauge, wrote a series of booklets to help us understand congregations based on their size. For over two decades we put all our eggs in the basket of the *church size* movement.[26] Rothauge proposed that we place our churches into distinctive size categories, believing that congregations of different sizes are organized in predictable and particular ways. Rothauge called these categories pastoral, program, and corporate.[27]

Although Rothauge cautioned that "other variables, such as context, available resources, local history, institutional and systemic cycles" were important, all anyone heard was that everything is measurable by size. This is now part of our normal way of discussing congregations. The size names themselves are part of our church vernacular. I have bought into this idea of categorizing churches for years. Rothauge had an idea—that there is a set of sizes and each size has a way of behaving. At the time, it produced some interesting ways of reflecting about our congregations. The problem, I have learned, is that Rothauge, and I when I used his material, created an observation bias.

Quantum physics and the observation paradox help us understand that no one observes the world without bias and without affecting the congregation by the observation itself.[28] It wasn't that he simply scientifically observed size, he and others actually created categories and influenced behaviors in particular ways—not all positive. Our desire to categorize and measure actually loses or dismisses important information about the congregation. We not only have a bias, we create an observation dilemma. If we think about it for a moment, what we realize is that Christian communities have actually functioned in different models, with different numbers of people participating for different lengths of time, with different economic models, and different leadership styles for millennia.

You see, Rothauge had indeed made a brilliant discovery. A congregation of 150 was not like a congregation of 500. This is true. Before Rothauge we'd tended to think about all congregations in the same way. Rothauge, however, believed that size was a primary way to think about congregations. I cannot emphasize enough how important and revolutionary this understanding was for us all. However, when Rothauge dismantled one observation bias he created a new one. To grow, Rothauge believed, you had to act like the next size up.

The observation bias created by Rothauge's work was that all congregations of the same size are the same. We have been using this model for years because we thought it was the best way of seeing congregations. But after over twenty years of ministry, and ten in a diocesan office, I know that is not true. All congregations are different, based upon the people who are in them, the place they inhabit, the cultural context in which they find themselves, how many people attend regularly, how old the congregants are, how much they give, and style of worship. This is one group of factors, and we could add many more, that create a multiplicity of effects that make the congregation uniquely who they are, healthy and unhealthy. Today in the Diocese of Texas we say when you see one congregation you see one congregation.

Margaret Wheatley thinks that we make a mistake when we discover a concept that works well in one area of an organization and then apply that concept to every area of the organization.[29] Wheatley writes, "All living systems change all the time as they search for solutions. But they never act from some master plan. They tinker in their local environments, based on their intimate experience with conditions there, and their tinkering results in effective innovation. But only for them."[30]

This does not discount the sharing of ideas and learnings. The future Church will share and invite with room for applied and contextual innovation. Wheatley writes, "Information about what others have invented, what has worked elsewhere, can be very helpful to people elsewhere in the organization. These stories spark others' imagination; they help others become more insightful. However, no premade model can be imposed on people. The moment they leave home, where they were created, they become inspiration, not solutions."[31]

Something else has been a product of our twentieth-century desire to measure everything. Our focus on size has ground into our denominational thinking the notion that Sabbath attendance—all ages, all Saturday evening or Sunday worship services combined, over the whole year—is the best single indicator of size for Christian congregations. The second of Rothauge's observation biases is that he based congregational health upon a model of what a church should look like that is now obsolete. The success or failure of mission should not be based on models that no longer exist. The future Church will have a diversity of models, not four. Effective small communities can crowd-source funding, meet at different times, for different purposes, in public or private spaces, and create their own church economy that is completely outside the model of church size. Small communities can be successful in new and different ways and are not prisoners to a prescribed way of being based upon their size. The healthy, thriving Christian communities of the future will be measured by their impact on the local culture and how well they are integrated into their community.

San Mateo, Houston, the fifth-largest congregation in the Episcopal Church, is full of life. It has over 1,200 people on Sunday, one priest, very few programs, and a full ministry, which is evangelistic and service-oriented. It does not fit any of Rothauge's concepts of a corporate-size congregation. St. Matthews, in the small Texas town of Henderson, has a bivocational priest, who is known throughout the community as a gifted pastor and teacher. Despite the fact that it is small, it operates with life and vitality outside of the chaplain model offered in its size description. It is mission- and service-oriented, engaging the community outside itself.

The Diocese of Texas and the Episcopal Church have congregations that are breaking Rothauge's church-size model. Even though we try and fit churches into the Rothauge boxes, and move them as they grow and shrink, we find that they are living organisms and don't fit. They have a complex life outside the box. It isn't about seeing what's in the box as alive or dead, it is about seeing that the church is alive and mostly outside the boxes we have created. When we think about churches only by their size, we end up trying to re-create something that may not have ever existed.

What the present church has inherited as the view of ourselves and how we are to proceed from this point forward is flawed. In the end, we can only see in part and know in part what God is doing. We must let go of a number of things in order to frame our future conversation. We must let go of our categories, our measurements for success, our narrow leadership job descriptions, and our economic models for doing church. In other words, we must let go of the core belief that this is the way it has been and this is the way it will be.

Margaret Wheatley writes, "Life is about creation. This ability of life to create itself is captured in a strange-sounding new word, autopoiesis (from Greek, meaning self-production or self-making). Autopoiesis is life's fundamental process for creating and renewing itself, for growth and change. A living system is a network of processes in which every process contributes to all the other processes. The entire network is engaged together in producing itself."[32] We must see differently, with new eyes, and work differently, with new ideas, if we are to allow for a living, thriving, autopoietic church.

Such a church will be a place with a perspective based outside its walls. We are invited by Christ and the Holy Spirit to leave the building and go out into the world. The church in the midst of the city of the living God will have to be gentle and meek as it steps out of the shadows. The church will have to mourn with all sorts and conditions of people. The church will have to proclaim in word the commandments of our God: to love our neighbor as Jesus loved us. The church will have to show mercy as Jesus shows mercy. And the church will have to seek a nonviolent immersion with the world outside its walls no matter how persecuted it may be. We must be fearless in taking our place in the public square, throwing aside the notion that religion and faith is a private matter. Through invitation, partnership, and participation, we must transform our streets and public places as venues for liturgy in the life of the church beyond our walls.

Stepping out, looking around, and figuring out where we really stand, I believe that the most effective missionary and mission organizations will be those that are led by teams. They will be diverse ethnically, embracing the multiple languages and cultures we find outside our churches. Successful mission will be dependent upon blended leadership talent, blended ages, and blended communication styles. Most importantly, though, is that wherever there is ministry there will be investment in the local community. We believe, as Margaret Wheatley says, "Relationships are not just interesting . . . they are all there is to reality."[33] This will mean that just as the world around us is organically connected, so too our organization will have to be organic and rich with networks that connect us to each other and the world around us. We are going to have to let go and return to a very rich and diverse understanding of community life and growth.

In order to discover our new context, we need to look at the world around us and imagine how our cities offer a vision of an autopoietic church. We can see now the artifacts for our future.

## Discussion Questions

1.  Margaret Wheatley says that we are often "mired in the habit of solutions that once worked yet that are now totally inappropriate." In what specific ways does her observation apply to the Church?

2.  Do you think that ASA (Average Sunday Attendance) is a useful metric for today's church? Is it important to use metrics to gauge congregational health? If so, what besides a church's ASA might we consider measuring?

3. Bishop Doyle notes that "the very health of the whole organization rests upon the health and vitality of the smallest relationships." Do you agree? Why or why not?

4. Bishop Doyle discusses how the church slowly regressed from a relationship-centered living organism to an institution focused on professionalism and liturgical observance. What surprised you about Doyle's narration of how today's Church evolved? What feelings did it evoke in you? What questions did it raise for you?

5. If a congregation wanted to make an intentional shift from being program-centered to relationship-centered, what three pieces of advice would you give that church to aid them on their journey?

## Spiritual Exercise

Go online and watch Brené Brown's TED Talk, "The Power of Vulnerability" (http://www.ted.com/talks/brene_brown_on_vulnerability). After doing so, ponder the following questions: How does this video speak to our task of becoming a more relationship-centered Church? What insight does it shed on our instinct to categorize and measure the wrong things? How might a commitment to vulnerability lead to a renewed sense of mission and adventure?

*Suggested Passage for Lectio Divina:* John 17:16–25

## Suggested Reading

Nassim Nicholas Taleb, *Antifragile: Things That Gain from Disorder.* New York: Random House, 2012.

Margaret Wheatley, *Walk Out Walk On: A Learning Journey into Communities Daring to Live the Future Now.* San Francisco: Berrett-Koehler, 2011.

# 6

CHAPTER

# A Renewed Mission Field

Let us begin by looking at the urban environment. The church for many years has been focused overwhelmingly on the suburban environment for mission. We have ignored the signs of a coming urban mass migration. No matter what your observation bias may be, we are in a massive global population shift into the world's cities. Today over half the world's population lives in urban areas. We are becoming an urban world. We begin here because this is the place where we have the most opportunity to see the future and move into it.

When we think about cities we think about downtowns, office buildings, skyscrapers, and the like. We think about the infrastructure. So when we think about the church in the city, we think about the church building. But a city is made up of people. The problem with how we imagine our urban mission is the same problem many in the commercial world face—we forget it is about people and not structures.

We do not build communities to build church buildings. We do not do our diocesan work in order to maintain the infrastructure of the church. We are in the business of creating communities so that people may come together, creating a culture of sharing grace, to work and serve others, to play and celebrate life.

We have for too long created a system by which people support the church rather than the church supporting the people in making community. When we do this, we take power and energy out of the organization—we take life out of the organism. The only way to build a vital and healthy mission in the future will be to engage with people in real time, where they are, and to listen and work with them to create the new living church. Our platform of structure and polity needs to adapt to the world and the people around us and not the other way around. We are to be a people-led community with the organization/platform supporting the work, not an organization/platform that leads and is supported by people. This is a very important flip.

"Social media has created a new interface for the city and how its citizens interact with it," says a report of the future of smart cities.[1] If the church is going to be part of the city of the future, we need to be part of the smart city today. We will need to rethink our infrastructure and make sure that it is supportive of the people and their movements and gatherings instead of the other way around. We must be in their time and in their space, listening and traveling with them as the new urban communities grow and develop.

As more people are moving to the city, so then a new focus upon making the city inhabitable is taking shape. Designers, architects, and community developers are reimagining the cityscape. They are not necessarily building new infrastructure so much as they are recreating the spaces we inhabit. Anyone in a city center that has watched an old factory or warehouse be transformed into lofts, retail, and office space can testify to this reality. In part, it is because as people return to the urban landscapes, those thinking about life in these spaces are asking, "How might . . . existing downtowns be creatively retrofitted—re-inhabited, redeveloped, and/or re-greened in ways that are economically productive, environmentally sensitive, socially sustainable, and aesthetically appealing?"[2]

It's not just downtowns, however. Suburbs now comprise the majority—in land area, population, and economic activity—of our urbanized areas. More potential gain could be achieved by focusing on adapting our least sustainable landscapes, in suburbia, to transform them into more resilient, equitable, adaptable, walkable, transit-oriented, and more public-oriented places. June Williamson "wondered what was being done across North America with vacant big box stores, dead malls, dying commercial strips, traffic choked edge cities, outdated office parks, and aging garden apartment complexes."[3] Her book, *Retrofitting Suburbia*, is worth a look if you are a missionary in the urban landscape that is even now evolving.[4]

Our cities and suburbs are being remade, and we need to be attentive as churches in order to participate. We need to have our eyes open to the values and trends that are shaping life. We also need to see clearly where people are migrating and how they are living. So what is happening, and how are people recycling space to build a better community?

People are redeveloping the existing infrastructure left by failed big box stores. At our house we called them "safety stores" because as soon as you saw them, we believed people were comforted by their presence. We imagined a person might say, "We are okay. There is a Bed Bath & Beyond." Or "I was worried I didn't know where I was. Now I know I will be okay. There is a Starbucks next to a Home Depot. We are safe now." It is safe because you can see it, but it is also safe because you can go inside these stores and restaurants and know exactly where everything is, how and what to order. Now defunct big box stores and the old manufacturing buildings of downtown are being repurposed. Across the country these are being rethought, gutted, and remade into community centers, gyms, and health clinics.

In downtown Houston, the Episcopal Diocese of Texas Health Foundation now shares space with a spirituality center in what used to be a stationery/paper printing building. In the small town where I first served, I can think of two places that were once a giant furniture store and an electronics store. Today, they house a community college and a mental health clinic, respectively. Reclaiming big box stores, malls, and shopping centers for churches and church-run clinics and service centers is a way in which we can move back into once-diminished spaces that are now being repopulated. Sharing space with new community centers has potential for mission.

Another area of renewal is the greening of both urban and suburban spaces. In downtown Houston there is a huge piece of green space where people gather and play called Discovery Green. There are concerts and movies. One of the largest Easter Sunday services is held there, followed by picnics and other activities. In a neighborhood just outside of downtown an old train track has been retrofitted for a hike-and-bike trail. The old concrete bayous are being taken out, and new walking and biking trails will connect the outlying suburbs with the heart of downtown. Across the United States there is a movement to restore and reclaim wetlands and creeks long paved over.

How can existing congregations participate in reclaiming spaces? If we are near a reclaimed space, we can put in a prayer garden. In food deserts, we can create vegetable gardens. Christians care about the environment, so we are challenged to connect with those who are doing this work. Whether we are sharing a hike-and-bike trail through our property or helping a neighborhood create green space, this is an opportunity for community connection. It is the church's work both to help these shifts happen and to participate with our communities in creating healthier environments.

## Changing Demographics

Today, our Episcopal Church has a demographic that is considerably different from the general population. The U.S. population is 62.6 percent Anglo, 17.1 percent Hispanic or Latino, 13.3 percent African-American, and 7 percent Asian or other. The Episcopal Church is 86.7 percent Anglo, 3.5 percent Latino, 6.4 percent African-American, and 3.4 percent Asian or other.[5] The Episcopal Church today is closer to what our world looked like in 1960. Do you see the problem?

I believe that in the future, our church will reflect the demographics of its culture. This means that the growing majority of our mission field will be made up of a diverse population. Our communities will have to be multiethnic and multilingual. Those who lead will have to be bicultural and able to transfer between cultures. We will have to be culturally humble. We need to be a missionary Church filled with people who are willing to listen to others rather than pretend we know who they are and where they are from.

In our church we possess all the qualities needed to live and thrive in this new mission context. The Episcopal Church as a community, as a mission society, is not a closed system. It is always in relationship with the community around it. Our constant interchange of ideas shapes and forms us. Sometimes it is difficult to see this; when scientists observe the molecular world of a cell and observe autopoiesis, they have to use very powerful microscopes. Researchers William Hall and Susu Nousala point out that it is difficult to see how such systems work because we see only what we can see. We therefore have a hard time focusing on our participation with the outside world. Every system, whether social or organic, is porous. We are more often than not left only with a hint or idea of the resulting action rather than actually observing the event of autopoiesis as it is happening. The engagement with what is outside is a necessary part of organic life, especially if that life is to thrive. Autopoietic organizations are bounded, complex, mechanistic, self-differentiated, self-producing, autonomous, and porous.[6] Let us take a moment to apply these qualities to the church as a missionary society and understand where our learning edges are.

## Bounded

We are a bounded system. We have ways of understanding our parts and places within the system. We have orders of ministry; we have parts to play and roles to carry out. We are limited, though, because we have so narrowly defined these roles that we are not able to creatively use them for ministry and mission in our current context. Here is a great example. We will license a layperson to take one piece of communion bread and a sip of wine to one homebound or hospital-bound person. Yet we are unable to wrap our minds around how that same person might be sent out to share the same gift of communion with a small community of individuals. We license lay people to preach inside the church, but we do not use them to go outside the church to preach and teach in small communities.

## Complex

Human beings are very complex, autopoietic creatures, and we build very complicated organizations. We have gotten complexity confused with only one form of order, though. We have replicated this form, built upon committees and board structures, throughout our organization. While some of this is important and even necessary for the health of the organization, we are no longer pliable. We need to be a much more organic system so that we can organize at different levels and for different purposes. The old system was built around the idea of permanence. But we need to be able to organize for a short while and to dismantle our structures when we are ready for a new mission. We know how to form a church like we have done for over a hundred years. However, we are stuck in this model and must figure out how to create other forms of communities. Our definition of *church* is too limited.

## Mechanistic

We have a very machinelike set of interactions that manage the church. We have an exchange of financial resources. We have created forms of communication that are clear. We have policies and procedures that help order life. But we have not updated our business models to keep up with contemporary practices. We know about pledging and offering plates. People in our mission context, though, function on less and less cash and do most of their giving electronically. They like to give to particular things and have choices. How can we engage them to support our mission and communities?

## Self-differentiated

Hall and Nousala tell us that "system boundaries are internally determined by rules of association, employment agreements, oaths of allegiance to organizational rules, deeds, etc., that determine who belongs to the organization and what property it owns."[7] While the Episcopal Church has plenty of these, there are other qualities of participation and many more forms of belonging. Our limited view of this is part of what is cutting us off from the world around us. In a world where people defined themselves primarily as belonging to a group, our limited understanding of *membership* worked. In today's world, where *belonging* has a much broader understanding, our ideas around membership, participation, and belonging actually prevent us from more adeptly engaging people. It is as if our understanding of the membership boundary has so shrunk that we are no longer able to engage with many who quite simply think about their participation in organizations in a different way. In order to be a thriving autopoietic community, we will need to broaden the ways in which people can belong to our Church.

## Self-producing

We know how to make Episcopalians. We have a variety of classes, and we invite people to take them so that they can become members. We prefer indirect recruiting; we rarely invite people personally to attend. We make new members in baptism and confirmation, but we don't really train them in anything other than an old model of church. We also make Episcopalians the good old-fashioned way, by having babies. We are going to have to do better. One of the reasons an autopoietic organization lives and thrives is that it makes new members well. It is constantly creating new cells—new members. At the same time, those members are changing the organization. If the organization ceases to make new members, it ceases to have new energy, new ideas, and new creativity. Just like any living organism, if it does not have new members (cells), it is in the process of dying.

### Autonomous

Autonomy is the idea that the organization can stand alone and outlive any of the individuals that now make up the organization. Let's pause here a moment. The church is a spiritual body, and it is the family of God on earth. It encompasses the human being and yet is beyond any one individual. Therefore, the nature of church is to outlive any of the individuals now involved. However, we have become so focused on our church buildings that the infrastructure of the organization is endangered, and we need more and more people and their energy to survive. We are eating our people alive. We are consuming ourselves. If we are to be an autopoietic church, we will need to be one where local communities are autonomous enough to create and multiply themselves.

# Putting Them All Together

We have boundaries, but they keep us from doing mission. We are complex, but rigidly so. We are mechanistic, but not in a helpful way. We are self-differentiated, but exclusively so. We are self-producing, but not at a sustainable rate. We are autonomous, but codependent. We have the DNA for autopoiesis, but we are misusing it. Why? Because we are stuck in a model that doesn't work.

In 1962, children were hiding under their desks in America, practicing for what seemed likely—a nuclear attack from the Soviet Union. Both countries were trying to figure out how they might survive an attack or if they should attack first. Hawks on both sides of the world were sure they had the answer. I believe we probably are not fully aware of how close we came to an extinction event.

One of the issues for the United States was how the leaders would speak to one another, post-event. The RAND Corporation was working with the military on a number of projects at the time. They had a man in their office named Paul Baran, who went to work trying to figure out this problem. His solution was to build a "more robust communications network using 'redundancy' and 'digital' technology."[8] Centralized and decentralized networks could easily be disrupted, so he created a distributed system of communications. Through the system, information is carried from one node to another on its own. Each node, while still part of the unit, acts autonomously and independently. It receives the piece of information, stores it, and sends it along to the next node. If there were a problem with one of the nodes, the information could take another route to its destination, as seen below.[9]

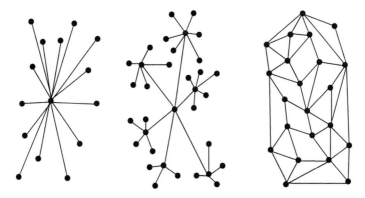

**Figure 1.** Illustration of Centralized, Decentralized, and Distributed Networks (Baran, August 1964)

*Wired* magazine interviewed Baran in 2003, and he talked about the system he had created: "Around December 1966, I presented a paper at the American Marketing Association called 'Marketing in the Year 2000.'[10] I described push-and-pull communications and how we're going to do our shopping via a television set and a virtual department store. If you want to buy a drill, you click on Hardware and that shows Tools and you click on that and go deeper."[11] When, in 1969, the RAND group founded ARPANET (Advanced Research Projects Agency Network) for scientists to share information, they could hardly have imagined the vast expanse of social and commercial activity that is today networked globally by the click of a button.

Baran's work changed the world we live in. What kinds of churches will we see living and moving in this world? What kinds of communities will reach the multiethnic, multilingual people who inhabit our mission context? How will these congregations inhabit the suburban and urban environments of tomorrow?

Let's apply Paul Baran's concept to the church. The church that we have inherited is built on a centralized model. People come to a central point—the church. Here they are ministered to and here they receive pro-grams and sacraments and pastoral care. Sometimes the priest or ministers will travel out to the parishioner's home or to their workplace or hospital. It is, by and large, a centralized model of community, which itself may have several levels of similarly working parts.

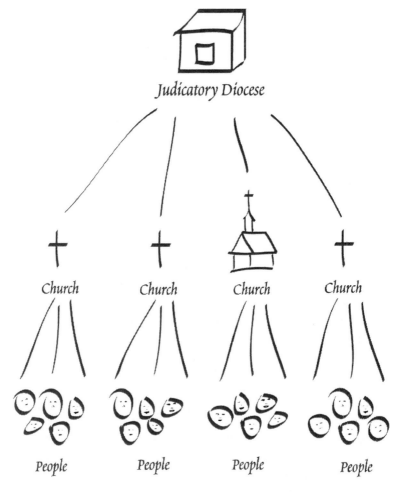

**Figure 2.** Current centralized Church model

We have made strides toward becoming more decentralized, primarily at the higher levels of the organization. But we are, overall, a weak organization because we still believe that everyone must come to the same center. When that center is disrupted (for whatever reason—and there are many), the system is put in peril. In order to truly engage the culture, we are going to need a distributive system of mission.

A distributive system of mission creates multiple communities connected together. These communities are of different kinds and they do different things. They share information through their own webs of connections. A distributive mission doesn't store everything in one place. In other words, a distributive system is not a bunch of centralized systems connected. It uses what it needs within the particular context of ministry. It then shares with others what it learns and receives from others what it needs to be successful.

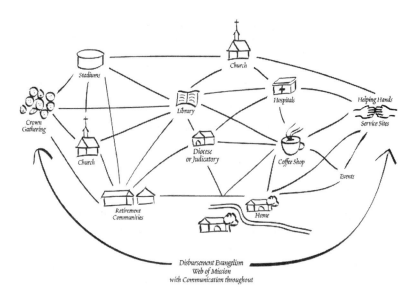

**Figure 3.** A distributive model of a networked future Church

# A Church Connected

When I graduated from seminary in 1995, we expected big churches to get bigger and small churches to die. That is not quite true today. Every church and every size is going to have to move to a more distributive model as part of the web of relationships throughout its context. In the future we will still have churches like we have them today. They will be of every size. However, they will be connected—each a network node within a larger church-wide system, indeed each a network node within a worldwide network. Large churches will have moved into a mix of ministries that are decentralized and distributive all across the city. They will be running multisite communities in people's homes, in retirement communities, in other church spaces, in rented spaces and office buildings. If these large congregations are to survive in the coming decades, they will have to figure out ways in which to connect with their members out in the world.

While the Episcopal Church has largely abandoned college campus ministry over the last two decades, it is time to reengage. This is one of the prime mission contexts for the future Church. However, campus ministry cannot look like youth ministry for college kids. Instead, the future of campus missions will follow the distributive mission model. No longer will students find their way to a campus center where the one campus missioner works. Instead the campus mission, like the networked church, will have nodes of connection throughout the campus and its surroundings. A mission at a tier-one school might actually start ministries at local community college campuses as well. The future Church no longer sees campus mission as a secondary isolated ministry for kids but as a primary mission site where the gospel is shared throughout the community.

We will also see the proliferation of small communities in this new distributive model. We will see house churches in urban, suburban, and even rural areas. Some of these will be connected to the larger church community as mentioned above. However, many more will be stand-alone. You may have one missioner priest with a team of lay leaders overseeing twenty or more of these small communities.[12]

In the future, the Episcopal Church will be many kinds of churches. We will have cyber churches, which gather online and share information and news, but do not have permanent meeting places. The cyber church of the future will use the distributive model of ministry to connect nodes of ministry in space and time throughout the community. It will be a church that uses different public spaces for worship, teaching, and Bible study. It will adopt other service ministry sites for its outreach. Participants will be connected through the Internet to each other, sharing prayers, thoughts, and experiences. They will find out the community schedule and go to a coffee shop for a Bible study, meet in a park for prayer and meditation, and work at a local clinic serving the poor and those in need.

Service communities will be another kind of church that emerges strongly in the next ten years.[13] These will be communities that rise up around particular ministries. We see this already occurring where there is an outreach to the poor or to those in need following a disaster. Communities spring up. People choose to worship with those they are serving. A great example is the outreach of Trinity parish in Houston, which grew up around ministry to the homeless. They started serving Eucharist following Sunday morning breakfast. What first started as something that was done *for* the homeless is now something that is done *with* the homeless and working poor. People choose to make this early morning service the service they attend. The community does its own Bible study, is creating a pastoral-care ministry, and is becoming a mix of people of every ethnicity and every social stratum working together. I know of similar communities in Atlanta, Los Angeles, and Washington, D.C.

Monastic communities will spring up as a revitalized part of the church's mission. In the Episcopal Church we already have a service corps whose chief hallmark is living together in community. Focused on a ministry of service, they follow practices of daily prayer and Bible study. They have a chaplain who mentors and watches over the community's life.[14] Other communities simply share a common rule of life. The Missional Wisdom Foundation operates a network of distributed but connected new monastic communities in North Texas. Small groups of individuals choose to live together under one roof and one rule of life. They participate in the community. We are now talking about how these same models might be adapted for people in their senior years who would like to live with others.

Many individuals will find community life by participating in "dialogue forums,"[15] where people gather in small groups to talk about spirituality or discipleship or to read the Bible. They will take place in people's homes, in coffee shops, in condominium community spaces, and in restaurants. Every church will need to be doing this kind of dispersed mission in the future. Individuals are going to look for spiritual opportunities closer to home or closer to their workplaces, and such communities will be an important way in which community life is engaged outside of the parish. It literally creates new doors into the community. Many people who are not attached to a community will find it much easier to be invited to and connect with communities like this. This is going to grow and become an essential ingredient of regular community life.

A compassion cluster is a short-term community formed by those doing work focused on a particular crisis. Along the Gulf Coast we see these clusters pop up after hurricanes. People come from all over and participate in a community of faith that provides food, volunteer support, shelter, and showers for those being served and those serving. We saw this happen with those who went to help clean up and rebuild after devastating wildfires in Bastrop, Texas. During the Occupy Wall Street movement in New York, clergy preached and celebrated the Eucharist among the protesters. At events such as these, people bring their desire for community and worship with them. Compassion clusters are opportunities to reach out, serve, and get to know others.

Small groups and prayer shelters will continue to multiply. Some of these read books together, while others have developed a practice of praying together. The individuals in these small communities may belong to other faith communities, or they may not be affiliated with any. They are primarily based upon friendship models. Throughout the 1970s and 1980s, Episcopal Cursillo reunion groups served as a way to organize the growing popularity of this kind of mission. They were essential to the growth that was seen during those years. They began to fizzle out for the same reason as many ministries—they became institutionalized. Such groups, however, have the potential of undergirding a distributive missionary system.

Another community that will be part of the distributed autopoietic mission strategy is the "marketplace ministry." Some companies have chaplains on staff to help care for their workers. However, such services are being dropped as corporations cut costs. Hospital chaplains are also going by the wayside as the cost of health care goes up. The Church, therefore, must engage in these places. We need to send lay and ordained people out to be with people in the places where they live and work. We still have a mission in these places, even if we do not own them or we are not paid. These are the many and varied places where the people are and where God is. They can be, therefore, important parts of our distributive mission focus.

This is not a complete list of the future Church's communities. There will be more kinds of Christian communities created by future missionaries that we can't even imagine today, but that will be intimately tied to future cultural contexts.

These many and diverse kinds of communities will be essential as large congregations step out into a distributive system of organization. Some congregations may leave their buildings behind and engage in one of these new forms of community, while others may transform their community into a monastery or service community. Regardless of how these forms are adapted and take shape, they will be the face of the new Episcopal Church.

This is a vision of a distributed network of communities across a geographic and mission context. They are visions of a living autopoietic organization that is bounded in multiple forms with the nature of belonging being shaped by the type of community. The diversity and multiplication of these forms will build a strong, healthy, and complex system. Each of them will be self-differentiated, not unlike individuals within a wide web of social relationships, but they will all be connected to the Church. The Church's current mechanisms will need to be retooled to provide for these new visions of church life. New forms of leadership and new freedoms will allow these congregations to be self-producing, self-replicating, and autonomous. They will adapt and change as they engage in their mission context with real people on their spiritual pilgrimages.

## A Dissipative Moment

Some say the church is dying, but I am unconvinced. Rather, we are living and ministering in a dissipative moment. Ilya Prigogine, a Nobel Laureate in Chemistry, helps me with this idea. He won recognition for his understanding of a new concept he called "dissipative structures."[16] In nature there is a contradictory reality, and that is that disorder can be the source for new order. Margaret Wheatley explains: "Prigogine discovered that the dissipative activity of loss was necessary to create new order. Dissipation didn't lead to the death of a system. It was part of the process by which the system let go of its present form so that it could reorganize a form better suited to the demands of its changed environment."[17]

Our problem is that we in the Church are formed by a perspective that is rooted in Western science. We believe that entropy is the rule and that if we do not constantly work harder and harder to keep pumping energy and resources into the system, then the system suffers from entropy—it loses steam and dies. Yet even now life is flourishing and new life is being born. Of course, you immediately can see that this is a biblical understanding, but as Episcopalians, sometimes it is easier to see it through the eyes of science.

Prigogine offers that in a dissipative organization those things that interrupt and interfere are essential to the health of the system. The system receives the communication and decides if it is to respond, change, or ignore it. Change happens either way. If the disruption grows so that the organization can't ignore it, then transformation and rebirth are possible. Wheatley says, "Disorder can be a source of new order, and that growth appears from disequilibrium, not balance. The things we fear most in organizations—disruptions, confusion, and chaos—need not be interpreted as signs that we are about to be destroyed. Instead, these conditions are necessary to awaken creativity. . . . This is order through fluctuation."[18]

We are in a dissipative moment. We cannot ignore the flotsam and jetsam of the future that is even now washing upon the shores of the Episcopal Church. We can see partly what will only become clearer in time. We have for too long suffered the sin of trying to get it right, and the shame of coming up short. But in a dissipative era we must have a greater sense of process and participation and experimentation.[19] If we are to move outside of our centralized structures and old exoskeletons, we must shed our skins and put on new ones. Jesus says, "No one puts new wine into old wineskins; otherwise the new wine will burst the skins and will be spilled, and the skins will be destroyed" (Luke 5:37ff).

A new urban and suburban world is emerging. We will continue to see people move toward the cities of the future. What we are experiencing across the Episcopal Church is globally true. People are entering city life by the millions and will continue to do so for a long time to come. The shape of our cities and the multiple possibilities for Christian community are before us. We have an opportunity. The question for us as we stand in this dissipative moment is, will we shrink from the challenge or face it?

It is important for us to see clearly the changes that are already affecting our congregations and communities in order for us to see the future that is before us. It is time we step into the future and begin to plant these new communities. What will they look like and how will they make their way into the new missionary age? The Christian in the new millennium will bring new challenges and opportunities. For us to be successful, we will need leaders who are digital natives and who can act within this new world. We need different kinds of leaders, and we need to rethink ways of forming and training leaders. This particular task will require that we revisit how we raise different vocations within the community. It has been given to this generation to undertake the dissipative moment and to answer these questions. We are a living church with a vital and necessary mission in the world.

## Discussion Questions

1.  Bishop Doyle says that we have "created a system by which people support the church rather than the church supporting

the people in making community." Do you agree with his observation? Why or why not?

2. Consider the church you currently attend. What space has been or could be "repurposed" to create what Doyle calls "a culture of sharing grace?"

3. Bishop Doyle says that the church needs to rethink "our ideas around membership." Is it possible to "broaden the ways in which people can belong to our church" while at the same time maintaining an emphasis on the necessity of baptism? Why or why not?

4. What do you think the difference is between a centralized network and a distributed network? Do you believe that the future Episcopal Church will embrace a more distributive model?

5. "The Episcopal Church is dying." After reading this chapter, in what sense is this statement true? In what sense is it *not* a true statement to say that the church is dying?

## Spiritual Exercise

Go online and find a distributive model of Christian community. Spend time on their website taking special note of how people connect, serve, learn, give, worship, and pray. After doing so, draw a diagram of the various interconnections and pathways by which information flows. Use Figure 3 from this chapter, "A distributive model of a networked future Church," as your guide. If you cannot find a distributive model of church online, you are free to create your own "future" church. However, if you create a distributive church in your mind, we encourage you to take steps to re-create that same church in the world!

*Suggested Passage for Lectio Divina:* Mark 9:33–41

## Suggested Reading

Stanley Hauerwas and William H. Willimon, *Resident Aliens: Life in the Christian Colony*, rev. ed. Nashville: Abingdon Press, 2014.
Reggie McNeal, *Missional Renaissance: Changing the Scorecard for the Church*. San Francisco: Jossey-Bass, 2009.

# 7

........................................................................................

# Into the Cloud of Unknowing

Sometimes I wonder if Richard Feynman[1] was looking up at the sky when he connected Bohr and Heisenberg's atomic model with the heavenly white fluffy mascarpone shapes we call clouds. Feynman was an American theoretical physicist specializing in quantum mechanics. He received the Nobel Prize in Physics in 1965, sharing it with Julian Schwinger and Sin-Itiro Tomonaga, for his work in electrodynamics. He was a member of the Manhattan Project team and later an investigator on the Space Shuttle Challenger disaster. For our purposes, he is the man noted for coining the phrase the "electron cloud."[2]

In science class in the 1980s I learned about the atom with brightly colored pictures that showed atoms clearly defined with an electron orbiting around the nucleus. Feynman describes the location of the electrons in terms of probable regions with fuzzy boundaries—like the puffy outlines of a cumulous cloud. The exact place of an electron just can't be determined.[3]

The largest objects subject to Newtonian physics have a more predictable pattern. Not so in quantum physics. All the quantum physicist can say is, "It is kinda over there . . . it is probably in this area over here."

When you take the flat model and turn it into a 3D model, it looks even more like a cloud. These areas are called orbital regions. It is like a little cotton ball—the puffy kind we used to glue to Popsicle sticks and turn them into sheep in Sunday school. The truth is that the electron cloud is unknown.

When I was an undergraduate, an American Orthodox priest taught me meditation and the art of contemplative prayer. We prayed together, and we read a book entitled *The Cloud of Unknowing*, written by an unknown Christian in the fourteenth century. Like an early quantum physicist, the author offers that the only way to meet God is to abandon all that you think you know about God and enter the cloud. The true disciple must have courage to enter the unknown without all the propped up ideas and certainties of definition. One enters the cloud of unknowing, and the heart is brought into union with God.

The author writes:

> For he can well be loved, but he cannot be thought. By love he can be grasped and held, but by thought, neither grasped nor held. And therefore, though it may be good at times to think specifically of the kindness and excellence of God, and though this may be a light and a part of contemplation, all the same, in the work of contemplation itself, it must be cast down and covered with a cloud of forgetting. And you must step above it stoutly but deftly, with a devout and delightful stirring of love, and struggle to pierce that darkness above you; and beat on that thick cloud of unknowing with a sharp dart of longing love, and do not give up, whatever happens.[4]

The work of the contemplative is to leave the world of certainty behind and venture into a cloud of uncertainty. I was once on a mountain in Colorado when a cloud engulfed the mountaintop. Moist, invisible visible droplets, cold and mysterious; my whole skin tingled. The disciple of God ventures into the cloud with its mix of observable reality and its mysterious invisibility.

The story goes that Jesus ascended into a cloud. Byzantine Christians built a church in the year 390 on the Mount of Olives called the Chapel of the Ascension. I went there—the clouds were low and hung above the treetops. The whole area is a sacred place where pilgrims pour in to see the place where Jesus, forty days after the resurrection, ascended into heaven. He did this as the clouds descended, making their way across the Jerusalem valley and engulfing him. Jesus is unified with God in the cloud of unknowing.

If we wish to follow this Jesus, to be disciples, we must abandon the security of the current structures of our church and walk bravely, courageously, into the future—into the cloud of unknowing. It is in this cloud that we will meet God. To cling tightly to our structures will keep us rooted in the swiftly fading past.

The future of the church will not be about a church, or a church building, but about creating Christian communities. The distributive model of church will mean smaller communities. We will be robust and stronger in this cloud model of mission. Today we are fragile because we have a model that says go big or go home. I like big, but if we become a church of a few large churches, we will have actually succeeded in becoming a more fragile organization. Everything breaks, and when the large community breaks, great is its fall. By engaging a missionary model that simulates the cloud, we will create a system of small batch communities that generate, regenerate, live and die, riding random events and the unpredictable economic and societal shocks that shake larger, more fragile communities.

We will need a church filled with people who, like quantum engineers and tinkerers, are willing to build smaller, more diverse communities. As leaders we will need to reject what Nassim Taleb calls a "fragilista" lifestyle—one that is afraid of fragility.[5] Our observation bias is that a larger congregation is less fragile. Our model is to build bigger and bigger congregations thinking that will protect us from fragility. This is the fragilista mindset. Taleb is saying when you put all your eggs in one basket you have actually created a more fragile organization. Taleb warned the financial sector that the 2008 economic crisis was coming in his 2007 book *Black Swan*. Applied to the future Church, a diversity of Christian communities will make our mission *more* antifragile.

Christianity is rooted in the mystery—the *mysterium tremendum*, the tremendous mystery—that is God. The unknown God speaks to us from in the midst of wild places. We are a people whose story is told at fiery bushes, mountaintop encounters, and desert voices of fire and storm. God speaks from a cloud and says of Jesus, "This is my Son with whom I am well pleased." Today we have become a people who avoid things we don't understand and cling to certitude, and it is killing us.[6] The Church is in need of mystery, the cloud, and a willingness to be fragile—a willingness to step outside the box—no, even destroy the box itself—and allow some parts to die and some to be reborn.

Our current church is a complex system that believes that we will be resilient if we have the right set of policies and procedures. We have all become fundamentalists—we are fragilistas. We are clinging to liberal and conservative casuistry,[7] attempting to legislate our organization one way or the other. In the process, we continue to create a more and more fragile system. It is no coincidence that as our canons and our canonical structures have grown, our church has become more broken and vulnerable to the VUCA world around us. Our longing for predictability and order is a rejection of a God who sends Abraham from the Land of Ur of the Chaldeans, who sends Moses into the wilderness, who calls prophets and sages to speak from the mountain caves to the people in their cities, who destroys temples and governments, who brings down Babel, and who brings about Pentecost.

If we are to have a thriving missionary church, we will need to spend time cultivating people and communities that live in the midst of the cloud of unknowing. There is a "cluster" of qualities that are needed by our church if we intend to be successful and antifragile in our mission.

Christian communities will vary and deal with internal variability—we will no longer be a church of programs that all have a curriculum and work in the same ways.

Our organization will need to be able to work with imperfect, incomplete knowledge and be willing to shift as we have glimpses of understanding, recognizing that we do not see nor comprehend the vastness of the possibilities before us.

We will relish chaos and enjoy the thrill of riding the energy created.

Our communities will seek opportunities that appear in the midst of changing cultural norms and attitudes, and use these for conversation and communication about who we are.

As a church we will be more disorderly, and able to adapt to the people and gifts that make up our communities.

We will reward innovation.

When there is turmoil or stress, we will use these as opportunities to discover and be challenged rather than as opportunities for anxiety.

Failures will be seen as learning moments, and time will be taken to ponder the reasons. Adaptability will be an intrinsic value in the system.

While Christian communities will be dispersed, they will also be cells in an interconnected network of communications, sharing learnings and outcomes. In this way the whole system benefits from the dispersal of creativity, experimentation, and engagement. This is the living Church of the future. The Church that does these things will become an antifragile Church and benefit in growth and viability, regardless of the cultural context.[8] The Church that exemplifies these characteristics will be a Church living its mission within the cloud of unknowing.

Today we have a fixed understanding of what church life is supposed to look like. Church life is nothing if it is not predictable. People come on Sunday morning to a service. Every church has a liturgy—a routine that is normative. People go to Bible study or Sunday school. There are seasons, and there are things that happen routinely throughout the year—Christmas pageants, stewardship drives, potluck dinners, and youth groups. There is very little randomness in our systems and programs. Consequently, we have been unable to adapt and change as people's lives have changed. The Church continues to believe that what we need is for people to change their behavior and go back to church attendance and a regularity of life that existed in the 1950s. This is not going to happen.

The problem is that the Church today is a large system, and large systems don't do small well, because small can't support all the organizational requirements of predictability. People become numbers, and as long as they are not disruptive to the system, they are welcome in it. We don't have time for the small or anything that challenges normal. Baptism, funerals, a hospital visit, Sunday school, youth group, and service attendance is about all we can handle.

There is a great deal shifting within the lives of our parishioners and the lives of people in our culture. We must work to see, and ask questions about, the smallest possible unit of relationships within the system. We will need to lean into the local and the tangible. In order for us to truly navigate the future, we need to realize that the future is about relationships. Without relationships there is no reconciliation, and without reconciliation we are not fulfilling our mission. This is the defining nature of our church's work.

When we invest in one person and build a relationship, the opportunity is opened to invest in their neighbors, family members, and community. This is called optionality.[9] This is how the first Christian communities grew. This labor-intensive ministry places the individual over the corporate desire for security and strength. Why? Because what we know is that the organization that seeks security and strength by using the rule of averages, the rule of canon, and the rule of repetitive systemic order will actually erode the relationship with the individual and create a fragile system.

The systems and focus of our church have created a world of religious tourists. They come into church in order to do churchy things. Then they leave for the other six days of the week not thinking much about their experience or how their faith might impact the rest of their working week. In the words of Taleb, we need to "detouristify" ourselves. What is true for organizations in Taleb's writing is also true for the church. As long as we are a church of religious tourists, we will lack the depth of relationships to truly transform the world. To understand this is to also recognize the difficulty of it and the reality that, as we currently do church, we don't have time for these relationships. Here is the beginning of wisdom.

## Discussion Questions

1.  What does "the cloud" represent to you? Are there any specific "clouds" that you have been avoiding? Can you think of a time when you encountered God in "the cloud"?
2.  What is the relationship between certainty and faith? Between security and faith?
3.  Leaders often boast when their church is "growing." Do you think we overemphasize congregational size as a barometer of health? Do you agree with Bishop Doyle that we must embrace "smaller, more diverse communities"?
4.  Have you ever experienced a deep failure that turned out to be an incredible learning opportunity? How might the church normalize "failure" so as to become a more adaptable organization?
5.  What does the phrase "religious tourist" mean to you? Have you ever been a religious tourist? How does the current structure of the church reinforce a religious tourist mindset?

## Spiritual Exercise

Slowly read Exodus 24:12–18 in a posture of contemplative silence. Read this passage as many times as needed to discern a word from the Spirit.

After doing so, use any artistic medium you wish—art, dance, poetry, song, etc.—to capture what you hear the Spirit saying to the Church.

*Suggested Passage for Lectio Divina:* Matthew 17:1–8

## Suggested Reading

Thomas Merton, *New Seeds of Contemplation.* New York: New Directions, [1949] 2007.
*The Cloud of Unknowing.* San Francisco: HarperOne, 2009.

# 8

# Communities of Service

John the Baptist believed that the essence of the Gospel could be summed up in this way: "Anyone who has two shirts should share with the one who has none" (Luke 3:11). A connected future Church is not meant to serve itself. In fact if it does, it won't work. We are called to do the work of caring on God's behalf in the world. We are to respond to God's love and provision of grace by in turn loving and providing grace through service in our communities. Jesus says a lot about the poor, and he is intent that those who follow him are to engage in service within and as part of their community.

The Gospels are clear and speak with one voice on the subject of service—Jesus believed that we were to serve our neighbor. Jesus makes it clear that, if we love him, he expects us to care for those who have been abandoned and marginalized, for the sheep who have no shepherd. What the Gospels teach is that we are responsible for the people in our lives and in the world around us. This work is more than just the rich tending the poor, though that is certainly part of it. Jesus's message goes beyond anonymous giving. It goes beyond charity for the sake of charity, which can actually do more harm than good.

The radical message here is that we care for each other, I for you and you for me. This moves us beyond the notion of a Samaritan helping out a beaten and abandoned neighbor or a rich man helping out a poor man. On the contrary, Jesus's message is that we are now part of a radically reconfigured family wherein each person is a brother and sister for whom we are responsible. This reverses Cain's answer to God's question, "Where is your brother Abel?" Cain, having killed his brother, then replied, "Am I my brother's keeper?" The answer from Jesus is, "Yes."

Through the cross, Jesus has taken on responsibility for us, for the whole world. Now he needs us to do the same, to take up our cross and follow, and care for the world. That makes us responsible for our communities, our cities, our states, our nation, other nations, and even our enemies. All the sheep are our responsibility.

Not just the ones who are like us.
Not just the ones who go to our church.
Not just the other Episcopalians.
Not just the Christians.

The hard lesson here, one we are all too eager as sinful, broken human beings to ignore, is that it matters to God how each one of us lives. It matters to God the manner in which we care for and stand with others. There is someone standing at the gate of our lives. And that person, that community, is waiting for us to stand with them as extensions of God's mercy, grace, and abundant love. This is not something that can be done on our behalf so we don't have to be bothered. A key and essential ingredient to the discipline of Christian life is that we are inconvenienced by the work of helping other human beings.

Christians believe that serving our neighbor is the way in which we incarnate God's love for all people. Episcopalians, when renewing their baptismal vows to God, promise publically to act on God's behalf in service to those in need. We respond to human need that stretches from our work together to help neighbors recover from natural disasters to helping our neighbors survive the human disaster of greed. We believe we are to work to transform unjust structures in society. We are invested in the work of sustainability and safeguarding resources because we live in God's creation. We are to renew the face of the earth and life upon this fragile planet.[1]

# Helping People Stand

The future Church, however, will engage in service differently than we do today. We will instead be a church entwined with the health and well-being of its community. God has a mission that engages the world through our feet, which take us to places that are forgotten. God's mission engages the world through our backs, which do the heavy lifting of rebuilding homes. God's mission engages the world with our hands, which are invested in lives and help people stand. The charity that has dominated our service ministries too often leaves people stuck in the same circumstances.[2]

In *Toxic Charity*, Robert Lupton writes, "Expenditures for a week of service by church and college groups are grossly out of proportion with what is actually accomplished. U.S. mission teams who rushed to Honduras to help rebuild homes destroyed by hurricane Mitch spent an average of $30,000 per home—homes locals could have built for $3,000 each. The money spent by one campus ministry to cover the costs of their Central American mission trip to repaint an orphanage would have been sufficient to hire two local painters and two new full-time teachers and purchase new uniforms for every student in the school."[3] This challenges our understanding. It is about the relationships, but if we cared about the work we might be able to create a different model of service.

Lupton introduced me to these words by French philosopher and author of *Money and Power*, Jacque Ellul:

> It is important that giving be truly free. It must never degenerate into charity, in the pejorative sense. Almsgiving is Mammon's perversion of giving. It affirms the superiority of the giver, who thus gains a point on the recipient, binds him, demands gratitude, humiliates him and reduces him to a lower state than he had before.[4]

The future Church will redefine the meaning of neighbor, as they become partners in ministry with those who live in their community.

Lupton offers an "Oath for Compassionate Service" that the future Church will take seriously:

1.   Never do for the poor what they can do for themselves;
2.   Limit one-way giving to emergencies;

3. Empower the poor through employment, lending, and investing, using grants sparingly to reinforce achievements;
4. Subordinate self-interest to the needs of those being served;
5. Listen closely to those you seek to help;
6. Above all, do no harm.[5]

The future Church will be a church whose individuals walk out of its doors and into the community and seek to know their neighbors. The living Church will be involved in and be a part of the community's strengths more than its needs. The individuals involved in this future service mission will be those who believe that the poor and those in need are indeed individuals with gifts and talents, with dignity of purpose, and equals. The future Church will be a church that is focused on its community context in its efforts to serve. It understands that each community is different—each congregation is different. The Church of the nineteenth and twentieth centuries became global; the Church of the new millennium will be a church that is local. It will intrinsically understand that a neighborhood is both a geographical location and a network of relationships. Service ministry in the future will be asset-oriented. It will build upon contextual strengths and resources rather than try to meet the need gap. It will see opportunities and be invested in creativity, imagination, and inventiveness. It will risk new things and encourage new partnerships and the creation of new networks.[6]

## Investing in the Community

Oftentimes churches today focus on issues they think are important. They decide, based upon their limited knowledge of the situation, and limited conversation with the poor, that they know what is needed and so set off to fix it. I have been in more than my share of these kinds of meetings. The future Church will be directed by the front-burner issues that the community itself raises. By building real-time partnerships with individuals in the community who are neighbors and in need, those invested in service will listen and hear the issues that most affect their new friends. The future Church will always be focused on the first issues first and then work toward the deeper and more in-depth issues as time and trust build. A living Church understands it is there as a partner in the community for the long haul. If people in our community care about safe public spaces, transportation, economic development, crime, or education, then God cares about these things, so the Church of the future, in a living partnership with the community, will care and join hands to create a well community.

The future Church will be an investor in the community. It invests therefore in economic development and partnerships. Loans, payment plans, and incentives are all used to empower those who are in need of creating a better living for themselves—they are never handouts. Along with the financial investment and time investment, service communities of the future will understand that they must be focused on increasing the leadership within their community. This does not mean *being* the leader but *raising up* leaders. "Indigenous leadership" is essential. Service organizations that are successful in the future will be those who empower, organize, and support local neighbors to raise their voices and do the things they did not think were possible. It isn't that we as a Church will help and be nice, but we will support them in doing the things we know they can do and achieve.

Lastly, the service community of the future will have a quality of patience. It will do its work with a long timetable. It will allow the service work to move at a pace comfortable for the whole community and not one based upon the needs of the Church. Progress will be measured based upon how the whole context and the people in the community take charge and begin to invest in one another's work and achieve the goals they have set out to achieve. It will not be based upon a budget requirement or vestry desire to see results.

Today what the church calls *outreach* has a few façades. If the church is large enough, they may have a person who helps organize where the money goes and how it is spent on local outreach projects. They may even organize groups to work in the community or go on mission trips. If the church is small, outreach is typically the project of a parishioner who has a particular passion or interest. So, the congregation in this setting takes on the work of the parishioner as their own: a crop walk, a local shelter, or perhaps a feeding ministry. These individuals, in the large and the small congregation, operate as a kind of program manager. These managers are responsible for motivating and organizing people within a larger system for the best performance. They are part of a hierarchy or power structure that is focused on fulfilling a charitable mission. I don't think this will end. The service ministry of the future Church will look more like community organizing than management.[7]

Individuals who are pioneers of networked communities and non-toxic service ministries are individuals who are today playing outside the church's *outreach* categories. They are individuals who have left the structure of typical nongovernmental, nonprofits, and churches behind and are now setting out to implement service strategies that are DNA for the future Church. They are uniting people in a room who share common values and share a desire to improve their community. They are connecting and networking in person and via social media. They are gathering people together—members and nonmembers. They understand that it is imperative to grow their group and build a movement. They invite individuals to participate and help build the service ministry.

The leaders understand they don't have all the answers or vision and must depend upon the group to help form and define their goals and aspirations. The leaders of the new service communities are advocates and supporters of the individuals involved. They are crossing the threshold of service organizations like churches and inviting leadership from all quadrants. In each scenario they recognize that because they are all working together to solve a common and shared issue, it is the social structure of the work that is important. So time and goals can be met and missed as long as the community is learning and building strength as a neighborhood family. A healthy community is their cause, and it is a cause worth working for and worth doing—without pay or other economic incentives. This is nonmonetary reciprocity. Centered in this entrepreneurial service is the fact that they celebrate being together, having built a commons and shared a common experience. The work is hard and the drive is internal but it is joyful and worth doing. The living Church of the future will be a community filled with individuals who are empowered to do this work inside and outside the church.

## Integrating Health and Spirituality

The future Church will be involved in shaping service as it integrates health and spirituality. The Church is interested in the whole person: body, mind, and spirit, so wellness is a perennial part of our ministry. We are a church interested in the way in which the person lives and moves within the broader community. In the past we have done this through hospital ministry (which the church owned) with resident chaplains. We have done this through philanthropy and outreach. The new era of health insecurity and the wellness of communities will challenge us to think in different ways. The church will be challenged to think about how it provides pastoral care and services to hospitals and the aging, living within communities (independent/assisted/nursing) without owning the facility. We must answer the call to missionary presence in these institutions. We have not done this, and in most dioceses across the continental United States we have abdicated our place in this particular part of our service ministry because of the health economy. The need is nevertheless present.

We will be challenged to understand that our communities may be access points for primary care and for mental health resources. As the culture investigates new ways to deal with health issues within the community, future congregations have an opportunity to be involved both in providing online connection tools and real space for clinics and in aiding the community to provide for its own health and wellness.

Churches of the future will be invested in their communities because they understand, first, that their own health is dependent upon it. In 2011, the *New England Journal of Medicine* reported on a study of the health of individuals who lived in low-income housing. What they discovered is that if we worked together on improving local neighborhoods, people who live there would be healthier.[8] There is a direct correlation between the community in which people live and their individual health. Jens Ludwig, the University of Chicago law professor who conducted the study, found that health outcomes changed based upon the kind of neighborhood in which people live. "The results suggest," he wrote, "that over the long term, investments in improving neighborhood environments might be an important complement to medical care when it comes to preventing obesity and diabetes."[9] When individuals work together to improve social structures, green spaces, access to health care, access to jobs, and a strong economy, the individuals who live in these places will actually be healthier and decrease the load on the wider public system. The future Church will be an active participant in building well communities.

The Episcopal Health Foundation of Texas (EHF) is a leader in redefining the future of service between the local church and its community context. We believe that in response to the future of service and community needs, the Church will be focused on building capacity in individuals, families, and institutions to enable them to create and sustain these well communities. Therefore it will invest in community development projects that incorporate health and wellness. It will support programs that build tenacity and resilience between the local church and the wider neighborhood in which it finds itself. The future Church will be interested in building capacity by partnering with local nonprofits already working in the neighborhood. It will focus on the real needs of neighbors with a special eye toward enhancing childhood development because of the long-term societal impact such investments will have.

Health care delivery can be improved by increasing access to high-quality, community-based preventive, primary, and mental health care. This will mean that the local church will partner with schools to help provide health care on site. It will use technology to expand access to care in churches, schools, and throughout the neighborhood in which it finds itself. It will help to integrate spiritual care with primary and mental health care. The future Church will help deliver more providers to underserved populations through shared space or collaborative funding.

Dioceses, local congregations, and nongovernmental organizations will work together to develop and sustain service ministries that work. The local church of the future will be invested in community-based research and development, ensuring that it is working on need-based ministries. The future Church will marshal its parishioners to volunteer and serve in a variety of settings. In order for the local parish to do this work it will have to train and organize its people and their neighbors.[10]

The future Church must be focused on long-term transformation. "Most charities take care of immediate needs. They are interested in finding the gaps in the social safety net and then filling them," says Elena Marks, president and CEO of the Episcopal Health Foundation. Our work, instead, has to focus our congregations on making lasting, sustainable change in their communities. Our service goal is to change the lives of our neighbors by adding intrinsic value. In this way we are able not only to keep them from falling into gaps, but also to change the world so that there are fewer gaps to fall into. We envision nothing less than a transformation of the relationship between the church, our parishes and institutions, and the wider community. The future Church must reinvent how our worshippers serve the communities in which they find themselves.[11]

This will mean that Church leadership at the diocesan level and at the churchwide level must support capacity building for the local congregation. Only by doing this can the Church hope to create strong human connections across communities. At EHF we believe that capacity building is a critical part of creating sustainability, self-sufficiency, and empowerment within communities, whether at the institutional, family, or individual level. Capacity building will play a critical role in how the future Church supports improvement in current efforts, as well as the development of new skills, new ways of working together, and new understandings of how we can be instruments of God.

In a transformed community, all groups are valued and participate in problem solving, including "the least of these." The future Church will understand that transformation also means that health disparities are reduced in the short term and root causes are addressed in the long term. The future Church that is engaged in service will build transformed communities where institutions and systems are aligned, integrated, effective, and sufficient for meeting the community's needs.

The diocese and the wider Church will have to be strategically focused on transformative community work if we are to be successful at changing how we do service. This intentional shift from charity to transformation will occur only when we change the way we fund service ministries. The future Church must think carefully and fund judiciously those projects that support the characteristics of a transformed community over the long term. We know that there are many factors that influence wellness, and that often they fall outside of our purview. Christian communities invested in transforming the places in which they find themselves will work alongside the populations they serve rather than simply "doing things for them."

After a local congregation chooses to do transformative service with its neighbors, sets its goals of interaction, and writes its oath for compassionate service, it must be strategic in stepping up its work intentionally. At EHF we believe that there are three levels of interaction needed to build the transformed community.

The first stage is investment in capacity building, strengthening partners and their impact. This means the first step is always to create better connections between the local congregation and their partners. The local congregation will work with other community members to build a common vision about the services that are needed.

The second stage will be to figure out, with community members, new ways for partnering and accomplishing mutual goals. The local congregation will work with other organizations and neighbors to figure out how to integrate their ministry, building conversations and leading initiatives that have a direct impact on the first-stage goals. The local congregation will continue to train and raise up partners to work with the neighbors, constantly fine-tuning its interaction.

The third stage comes after proven, sustainable structures and processes have been put into place. This means that there is a level of self-sufficiency for the service ministry; it organizes on its own; the next set of goals comes naturally through conversation and relationships. The local congregation can then export what it has learned and share the new model widely, so that the wider church at all levels benefits from the local work.

For this to work, congregations, dioceses, and national church leadership will have to commit to becoming learning organizations. This means continued evaluation, measurement of impact and work, assessment of internal/external organizational effectiveness, attention to new research and best practices, recognition of new opportunities for capacity building and training opportunities for all involved, and research on the changing context in which the community is working. This means that service is an iterative process—we are constantly reflecting on our work. Ultimately, this work will be an investment in the local church citizens to work with the local community to transform the cities where they live.

Recently my wife and I made a trip to San Francisco. We are garden lovers, and a friend recommended that we go to see the gardens just below Coit Tower by way of the Filbert Steps, a steep stairway on the east side of Telegraph Hill. The Steps provide the only access to the homes there, and the residents have covered the area with gardens. A feral flock of parrots even resides there. This is an example of an urban movement that is intimately tied to the creation of healthy communities. People are taking city planning and creating pedestrian-friendly blocks in a movement some are calling "pop-up urbanism."[12] Future Christian communities will be actively involved in such movements.

Part of what has happened is that city governments no longer have the ability to truly care for and support the transformation of public space. In the Houston area, we see many individual philanthropists, entrepreneurs, and foundations filling the breach. Churches can do similar work, but they also have the ability to partner with their neighbors in deeper ways, transforming their neighborhoods into well communities. Socially engaged and organized communities can undertake urban design without high public cost. Sometimes this work even changes the way in which the local municipality does their own work.[13]

The Better Block project was founded in 2010 in the neighborhood my parents grew up in—Oak Cliff in Dallas. Organizers raised $1,000 and used found objects and materials to change the community. Their goal was a "complete street."[14] Wikipedia defines a complete street as "one designed, operated, and maintained to enable safe, convenient, and comfortable travel and access for users of all ages and abilities regardless of their mode of transportation."[15] Together, members of the community organized, and they painted a bike lane and greened up the space with the help of a local landscape company. They used free space for a café, flower market, and art studio for children with a space for musicians to hang out. Today Better Block is all over the country and is an urban movement.

These grassroots community-improvement projects are called "tactical urbanism, pop-up urbanism, urban acupuncture — or in one blogger's ornate locution, 'Provisional, Opportunistic, Ubiquitous, and Odd Tactics in Guerrilla and DIY Practice and Urbanism.'" A New York design firm, Macro Sea, has even created swimming pools that can be moved into the area where no public recreation exists.[16] The goal is to integrate individual participation with community improvement for a lifestyle that is collaborative, creative, and participatory. They use social media, small house gatherings, social funding, and a host of other connection tools to organize people into actually making their community a better place to live. Responding to a Better Block initiative in Fort Worth, Deputy Planning Director Dana Burghdoff said, "It was inexpensive and fast. It mobilized public support for the city's ultimately successful effort to convince the state to reroute the highway. Two traffic lanes have been given over to on-street parking and bicycles, and plans are in the works for wider sidewalks, street trees, new lighting, and benches. South Main is once again just a city street."[17] These tactical urban strategies will in the future be intimately linked to the whole wellness initiative.

Remember the example of St. Luke's Methodist, the networked church in Houston that adopted the Gethsemane campus as a satellite?[18] Here is the rest of the story. As St. Luke's began the process of adopting the site, they needed to figure out what ministries might be done through there. They sent a layperson, Gene Graham, and one of their clergy, the Rev. Justin Coleman, to survey local neighbors, business owners, and community leaders to discover the needs of the Sharpstown area. It became clear that urban gangs were a big concern.

Graham and Coleman then brought in Charles Rotramel, founder of Youth Advocates in Houston. Youth Advocates is a nonprofit that works with kids to help them stay out of jail, in school, and making progress toward their goals by building relationships with mentors. Rotramel's work has changed the lives of thousands of Houston youth.

Rotramel then brought in Eric Moen, who specializes in bridging Youth Advocate groups with church communities. Moen is the director of urban ministry and mission at St. Martin's Episcopal Church. Together, this foursome developed a funding apparatus, built relationships with the county (judges, parole officers, police, and social workers), and launched reVision.[19] Today reVision is an ecumenical service ministry that was built from the ground up and pools charitable and government dollars to recreate the local community around the Gethsemane campus. Their mission statement reads: "reVision leverages the power of community by connecting kids on the edge with mentors, positive peers, and life-changing resources." Parishioners, young adults, and kids all work together to support one another. The collective theme of their stories is the transformation of life. This is a glimpse at the future of service ministry by engaged churches.

Stewardship and service is not the business of redistributing wealth, it is the business of building relationships. The reciprocity is not a financial exchange but one of story. We help people in our community by being their friends and by living into our real connection with them. The church is called to go out and proclaim a gospel that is more than just words. We have a mission field in our own backyard. We have a mandate from God to tend the fields at home; to walk out of our congregation and find out the needs of our neighbor, to introduce ourselves, to say we are here to help you, and to ask what does this community need? Then we must undertake the sweat labor it takes to help.

On our watch there exists a care vacuum. Millions have no health insurance. Forty percent of all emergency department visits are for conditions that could have been treated in a primary care setting. African American women's rates of breast cancer mortality are higher than white women's. Why? These women are less likely to get mammography screening and more likely to be diagnosed at a later stage of cancer. Nationally, one in five children suffers from mental, emotional, or behavioral disorders, but only one in eight of these are currently receiving treatment. "Food deserts" are creeping like the sands of the Sahara as a great migration moves to the cities where there is not enough access to healthy food. These food deserts result in higher rates of diabetes, obesity, and heart disease—and higher medical and insurance costs for us all. As the disparity between the rich and the poor grows, we are seeing more U.S. children grow up in "food insecure" households. Extreme poverty and the homelessness that often accompanies it decrease the life span of an individual by an average of twenty-five years.

God has a mission. God's mission has provided over the years missionary outposts. In these outposts are people who stand at the ready to make the neighborhood better, healthier, and safer. These are the things that matter to our communities. The church of the future, invested in the lives of the people in their communities, will be out holding and convening neighborhood conversations.

We are the church that says we are invested in the dignity of every human being—the future Church *will* be invested in every human being. We must dream. Dream with me about a mission that understands that health is a state of complete physical, mental, and social well-being, not merely the absence of disease or infirmity. Dream with me about lowering breast-cancer deaths for the poor and helping children find the care they need. Dream with me about unleashing the resources of people across our Church to bring health care to the poorest of the poor, health education to our neighborhoods, and public gardens that bring forth a bounteous harvest in what today are food deserts. We have the opportunity to be our neighbor's best partners, because as a church we know their problems and struggles are our own.

## Discussion Questions

1.  What about this chapter most excites you? What questions does it leave you with? What fears does it evoke?

2.  What is the difference between practicing charity and investing in community restoration? Which of the two is more difficult and why?

3.  Bishop Doyle says that the future Church will "integrate health and spirituality." Is it possible to heal one's spirit and leave their body and mind unchanged? Why or why not? What does it mean to heal the "whole person"?

4.  Think of the neighborhood in which you live. What communal needs do you notice? What types of people aren't thriving? What is one thing the Church can do to bring God's shalom (wholeness) to your neighborhood?

5.  "It is better to teach people to fish than to give them a fish." Do you agree? Why or why not?

## Spiritual Exercise

In this chapter Bishop Doyle lists the six aspects of Robert Lupton's "Oath for Compassionate Service." Think of an outreach ministry your congregation is engaged with. Using a scale ranging from 1 to 10, go through each of the six components of the Oath for Compassionate Service and rate how well your church is doing using Lupton's criteria. After doing so, think of one tangible way you can move this particular outreach ministry away from a focus on charity and more toward an emphasis on community restoration.

*Suggested Passage for Lectio Divina:* Matthew 14:13–21

## Suggested Reading

Robert D. Lupton, *Toxic Charity: How Churches and Charities Hurt Those They Help.* San Francisco: HarperOne, 2011.

Richard Stearns, *The Hole in Our Gospel: What Does God Expect of Us? The Answer That Changed My Life and Might Just Change the World.* Nashville: Thomas Nelson, 2010.

# 9

# Generous Evangelism

Service is the Good News of salvation put into action. Evangelism is the sharing of the Good News of salvation and the uniqueness of Jesus Christ with others. Mainline denominations have an easier time with charity than with service or evangelism. In a future of competing narratives and an abundance of communication, the gospel could get lost—but not for the future Church. The future Church will be alive and well and proclaiming a clear message of Jesus Christ and God's mission in the world. The Church will do so with clarity, because in a VUCA world, clarity is necessary. Bob Johansen writes: "The best leaders will understand why people crave easy answers, but they won't fall into the easy answer trap. Leaders must develop clarity while tempering certainty. Clear-eyed leaders will experience hopelessness on occasion, but they won't accept it; they will see through it and be determined to make it otherwise. Leaders will immerse themselves in the VUCA world and—even if they become disoriented for a while—make a way to clarity as they make the future."[1] We are a Christian enterprise. We have already been clear about our vision and understanding of God's mission. Evangelism is about the sharing of that vision.

# A Brief History of Evangelism

Evangelism, the sharing of the Good News of salvation and the uniqueness of Jesus Christ, has forever been part of the essential work of the Church. Jesus's first followers shared their understandings of his teaching, incarnation, resurrection, and ascension through stories and letters. The first three hundred years of the Church saw divisions, as varied theologies emerged about the person and meaning of Jesus, but Christians agreed that God was present in the workings of the world and it was their work to interpret God's presence and to work for the world in God's stead. They sustained a belief in the uniqueness of Jesus and their particular vocation when imparting this message to others.

There is not a lot of evidence about how people shared the faith with one another, but we can be sure they did. Rodney Stark in his book *The Rise of Christianity* notes these statistics: In the year 100, there were about 7,500 Christians; by the year 200, there were about 220,000 Christians; by the year 300, there were over 6 million Christians, and by the year 350, there were about 34 million Christians.[2]

One can imagine that this happened as described in the book of Acts: people shared with one another who Jesus was and how his resurrection and grace made a difference in their lives. Stark's text goes into the complex sociological reasons why this new movement might have gained a foothold; nevertheless, it did, and it took off, and pretty soon it was everywhere, beginning in households and then growing throughout towns and cities. Historians in general believe that it was as simple as that. Ordinary Christians talked about Jesus as humanity's certain hope. They "gossiped about the gospel."

The pagan Celsus, a second-century Greek philosopher mentioned by the early church father Origen, complained that "wool workers, cobblers, laundry workers, and the most illiterate and bucolic yokels" were sharing the story of Jesus and how God loves everyone. Origen mentioned that there were people traveling to different towns and cities—taking the idea of the great commission seriously—and sharing the old story with whomever would listen. By the middle of the fourth century Christianity began to supplant all the other religions and temples, and by 381 became the official religion of the Roman Empire thanks to Constantine's mother. Catechism, which had been a time of teaching for new Christians, was replaced by instruction in "ritual and custom." In fact, evangelism now began to fall away across the Roman Empire, as Christianity was simply adopted upon conquest. This was especially true in Armenia, in Germania, and with the Celts and Slavic tribes. The people became Christian because their leaders became Christian.

In the Middle Ages, it was the sword and imperial victory by Charlemagne, the Teutonic Knights, and the Crusades that spread Christianity. Saint Cyril translated the Bible into Slavonic, and the idea that people should be able to hear the word of God in their own language was born. What took place in the Middle Ages was a shift in who did the evangelizing. It was most definitely not the layman. It was the monk, the priest, and the bishop—serving as missionaries—who were sharing the Gospel in foreign lands.

This would last well into the twelfth and thirteenth centuries, when lay movements began to do what the others were no longer doing. There are, as in any short survey, exceptions, but this is the basic pattern. Lutheran professor Richard D. Balge writes:

> When some monks in the West returned to hermitism and others concentrated on the aggrandizement of the institutional church, a number of lay movements sought to do what the ordained churchman were neglecting to do. In the 12th and 13th centuries the Humiliati, Beguines, and Beghards were voluntary (but disciplined) lay people who cared for the bodies and souls of society's castoffs. Peter Waldo's followers went out two-by-two in the 12th century. They preached repentance, they distributed Bibles, they heard confessions and spoke the word of forgiveness. In England, in the 14th century, John Wycliff trained itinerant lay preachers. Hussites and a remnant of German Waldensians combined in the mid-15th century as the *Unitas Fratrum* to evangelize in Europe and to take the Gospel to Turkey, Syria, Palestine, and Egypt. Formally, none of these groups preached an unconditioned Gospel.[3]

Each in their own way shared a gospel across the reachable world: that God acted through Jesus and that God's love was sufficient, and they called upon all those who would follow Jesus to respond to this grace.

The next era in evangelism is characterized by two developments. One was the growth of monastic movements that sought to evangelize the growing colonies of the great countries, harkening back to earlier clerical missionaries. The second was the Reformation, which changed more than evangelism, of course, but had a powerful impact on how evangelism would be done. Martin Luther (1483–1546) said, "Every Christian is also an evangelist, who should teach another and publish the glory and praise of God." The confession of Jesus as Lord and Savior would be the hallmark of the Protestant movement. "The most aggressive of the 15th century 'left-wing' Protestants were the Hutterites. Stressing that every baptized believer has received the Great Commission, they evangelized where they were and sent missionaries to distant points in Europe, where some of them were put to death as heretics," Balge writes. During this great reform, the gossip of the gospel would be the primary medium—the poor, the household workers, the tailor, the weavers, the farmer, and the nobles would all be whispering about the power of God in Christ Jesus.[4]

John Wesley, George Whitefield, and the Moravians would join the colonists in a new world, expanding the idea of spreading the Kingdom of God. The First Great Awakening (1730) and the spiritualization of the gospel would take root in the American colonies. While revolution and war would come to Europe and the new world, evangelism was also taking on a new form. Individuals were again firmly in charge of offering the Good News. The poor and the worker were of concern, and the mix of service and the gospel is found in missionary societies. These societies were funded and supported by their respective denominations and communities.

The YMCA (1844) and the YWCA (1858) ministered to Civil War vets and urban youth. The Salvation Army (1865) went to the poorest of the poor. John Mott's World Student Christian Federation and Dwight Moody's Student Volunteer Movement recruited world missionaries and home evangelists. This would lead to a new spiritual awakening and a new global missionary zeal. By the 1950s, evangelism was firmly rooted in evangelical movements but was no longer an emphasis of the mainline denominations. The growth of the suburbs and the Baby Boom would bring great prosperity to the mainline denominations, and evangelism seemed unnecessary because so many were already in church. This was the height of the Episcopal Church.

By the 1990s, the denominational churches were trying to reverse the decline in Sunday attendance. The Episcopal Church declared it a "Decade of Evangelism." During this decade, the mainline denominations would shrink even more than in the previous ten years. People within denominational churches today are not especially interested in evangelism, and they are less likely than ever to share the good news of Jesus Christ with their neighbors.

As Christians, we must own the reality that the gospel has not always been an invitation or a benefit to those who heard it. For with the gospel has come a sinful broken Church. It has been an organization that sometimes has persecuted the people who were supposedly in their care. But the crimes and misdemeanors of the past, committed by those who abused the gospel, are no reason for us to dismiss our duty as followers of Jesus to share the grace and love of God. It is important, I believe, to recognize that when Christianity and evangelism were at their best, it was not typically the organized Church at work but rather people, simply people, sharing hope, grace, and a sense of transformation with their friends and neighbors.

## The Art of Evangelism

The future Church will use innovation and creativity to share the age-old gospel message. The bedrock ministry of the Church is teaching, baptizing, and nurturing those who choose to make their pilgrimage with Christ. Evangelism is a primary characteristic of a church that responds to the human need for the divine and the sacred. In the future Church, evangelism will be distinguished by lay-led sharing of the Good News.

Today, for-profit companies are investing in evangelism, transformation, and disciple-making. The chief apostle in the "church of the customer" is Guy Kawasaki. He invented a position for himself at Apple Computer as "chief evangelist." The for-profit sector has been using these terms and making disciples since the early 1990s. What happened in the Decade of Evangelism is that our terms were co-opted to sell stuff. Kawasaki's books, with titles such as *Selling the Dream: How to Promote Your Product, Company, or Ideas—and Make a Difference—Using Everyday Evangelism* and *Enchantment: The Art of Changing Hearts, Minds, and Actions*—are important resources if you are interested in learning how he uses the "E" word. Instead of debunking evangelism or rejecting the culture's appropriation, the future Church must reclaim it and use it as a point of introduction to the Christian faith. The Church must reengage and explain that the God we believe in doesn't want you to buy something. The God we believe in is a God of grace and is invested in our lives. Unlike the gods of the marketplace that demand product loyalty, our God gives free grace, mercy, and kindness. Our God forgives debt and debtors.

The gospel of Jesus Christ revealed in the life of a living Church can spread, and it will happen steadily, organically, and exponentially through what I call generous evangelism.[5] Generous evangelism is when our church, out of a sense of abundant grace, overflows its boundaries out into the world. Generous evangelism listens to others as they tell their pilgrim tales of seeking God in the midst of a wilderness culture. Generous evangelism takes place when people are willing to walk with other persons as they make their journey. It waits to hear about, and then names, Jesus Christ in the lives of others, revealing the icons and images of God acting in each person's life. It invites people into community. It welcomes them. It helps them to find a language (in our case, an Episcopal language) for entering the faith conversation. Generous evangelism is concerned with welcoming people into the family and bringing others into a sacramental life with God.

This renewed evangelism will take many forms, as diverse communities are inspired to be creative in God's vineyards. In existing traditional church contexts, generous evangelism will take the form of invitation and newcomer hospitality. These first steps will lead to a discipleship process, where people are formed through the sharing of our particular Episcopal way. They will become part of the community and be formed, and come to belief, as they chart their own pilgrimage and journey with Christ through the liturgy, Bible studies, and discipleship classes. In turn, they will help others find their way into relationship with God.

New Christian communities that sprout up around cultural commonalities or diaspora groups will also be important innovative centers of evangelism. Music, art, and shared expressions will bind these communities. The small-batch churches are communities formed in context and will have many diverse expressions in the years to come. Evangelism will take place in these regardless of what form they take. Even service ministries will have an evangelism component.

The Church of the future will have to launch many different kinds of Christian communities and be willing to use different styles of engagement with the culture. As we do this, our core teaching will have to be strengthened, not as the end-all–be-all of belief, but as a means to engage people as they make their journey into our church community. If we are to engage different people, with different life experiences, we will need to be prepared by being in touch with our own faith. This effort will be marked by communal discourse and be led by laity and clergy alike, in the church and more importantly out in the world.

The living Church will embrace a missionary spirit that sows seeds with wild abandon. It will sow seeds in places where there are birds, and sometimes it will have to shoo them away. It will have to be willing to pick up the stones so that the seeds may grow on the soil beneath. It will have to fearlessly sow seeds and gently care for them, protecting them from the weeds that will want to choke the tender shoots. Resources (both human and financial) will be needed for this work. Stewardship and development will be core strategies that complement the communal work of loving conversations and generous expressions of evangelism.

The evangelists of the future Church will burn with a clear and compelling message that brings good news to the world. The Episcopal Church has such a message. We believe that Jesus loves all people and that the Holy Spirit empowers us to spread God's love with the world. The Episcopal Church makes people's lives better. It battles poverty and works against injustice. The future Church will have many evangelists, because it will be filled with people who love their community. The spiritual interconnections that are made in Christian community become part of the fabric of life in the surrounding community, helping Episcopalians lead an integrated way of life. If evangelists do not love their Church and its proclamation of Jesus, they will not make very good evangelists. Let me see . . . how can I say this? If you think your church stinks, evangelism will not come easy to you. But the future Church will have many evangelists who love Jesus and the Church.

## Doing Evangelism Well

Here are some basic criteria for good evangelism in our current context. Good evangelists will focus their efforts on those who are looking for God, who are exploring Christian communities, and who are genuinely interested in a new spiritual experience. Guy Kawasaki says, and I agree, that a good evangelist knows within five minutes if they have a chance of success with an individual.[6] This has been true in my experience both in retail sales and as an evangelist. It is far better to focus on interested people who are curious about God than it is to try to convert people who are happy with their current Christian community or other faith or just not interested. The future Church works intentionally with those who choose to visit, choose to look around their website, choose to participate in their social media, and who ask inquiring questions. The evangelist will look for all of these opportunities and may in some cases create them. The evangelist remembers that those who used to be Episcopalians or who were part of the denominational church at one time or another are more likely to find something of interest in our Church. The evangelist always remembers that being kind and a good friend first is essential. The Episcopal Church that is thriving in the future will be one that is known for its hospitality, kindness, and helpfulness as people try to make their pilgrim journey. We hope most people will say, "We found the Episcopal Church and we loved it!" But when they discern we are not for them, we hope they will say, "It wasn't quite right for me, but the people there were incredibly kind and supportive of my spiritual journey." Evangelists are kind.

The evangelist must get beyond insider church-speak. The evangelists of the Episcopal Church and its gospel know that people may be interested in mystery but they are not interested in vocabulary they can't understand. These are different things. People are not going to choose the Episcopal Church because we have great hymnody and fantastic liturgy, because it's high church or low church. They will choose it because at the end of the day what the evangelist tells them is true—being an Episcopalian who loves Jesus makes a difference in your life. Guy Kawasaki says, "Macintosh wasn't positioned as the third paradigm in personal computing; instead, it increased the productivity and creativity of one person with one computer. People don't buy 'revolutions.' They buy 'aspirin' to fix the pain or 'vitamins' to supplement their lives."[7]

The Episcopal Church that is thriving in the future will be one that understands that while it has boundaries for community membership, it also has plenty of room for people to come and go and to test-drive that community. The Episcopal Church is meant for everyone, even though it may not fit everyone. For some visitors it will be a stop on the way to another faith community. The evangelizing community that flourishes in the future will be one that understands this, and instead of belittling those who do not choose it, will be the kind of community that trusts the individual's discernment. The masterful evangelist trusts the product and trusts the discernment of the individual to figure out if the church is right for them. The Church of the future will do what it does best—invites, welcomes, and connects people to others in and around the community.

The innovative evangelist will be able to talk about their community and why they love it so much. They have to be able to give a "great demo," as Guy Kawasaki says. They can't use sentences like, "I like the liturgy," or, "The priest is nice." Those are good qualities, but they really are meaningless to people on the outside. They might simply ask, "What is liturgy? And, you have priests? Do you have priestesses?" The evangelist knows that while they have the prospective person's attention, they have to help them experience the best of the Christian community.

First, the generous evangelist invites people to come to church. This is *key*. The generous evangelist actually shares their community with others by inviting them into community. This can mean having them join you for a worship service. But in the future Church, there will be many other opportunities for the individual to come and meet members of the community and to experience what God is doing there. At the end of the day, no matter how it happens, the generous evangelist will create opportunities to demo their Christian community experience. The evangelist of the future invites a newcomer to a great event—such as a performance or a discussion of a topic that is of interest to the visitor—and introduces him or her to good people in the community. The evangelist, by giving a demo, helps new people have a good experience and interpret their experience. Not everyone can give a good demo, but that is not the only part of evangelism.

The next piece is essential for the generous evangelist of the future— listening. I have been in retail sales and have over a hundred hours in mediation training and thousands in experience. Regardless of what the work is, it is always about listening. Sometimes leaders can forget to listen. The future Church and its generous evangelists must be good listeners. Generous evangelism is chiefly about transformation. Transformation begins when an individual comes to an understanding and recognition that the Episcopal Church can be a good addition to their lives because of its particular and unique presentation of God in Christ Jesus. The generous evangelist is not simply making a presentation of material but is inviting the other person to have a better understanding of themselves, God, the church, and others. This is not going to happen by simply being an evangelist who sells the gospel—if you will pardon my crassness. The generous evangelist listens.

The generous evangelist listens by asking questions and being quiet while the person answers or tells their story. But it isn't just about asking questions. Sometimes a pause in the conversation, a nod, and an invitation to continue will allow the individual to truly share their story. The evangelist knows and understands that what we are doing is weaving a common story, and that this common story only happens when all are given a chance to do some of the weaving. Newcomers must have the opportunity to see if their weaving will fit within the long woven cloth of the Episcopal Church.

As Richard Ruff, a sales consultant, reminds people, it is not enough to listen—the person you are listening to has to know you listened.[8] After all, listening is not an inactive occupation. While listening, an evangelist needs to test what they hear—make sure you have it right and give the speaker time to correct or add to what they have already said. You might summarize or reflect back to them what they are saying. Don't share your story unless they ask! Sharing too soon can tell the person that this is all really about *you*. Listen to how they are speaking about their experience. The qualifiers they use in their storytelling will give the evangelist an idea about what the individual thinks is important. Nonverbal signals are also an indicator, so pay attention to whether they are animated or not as they tell the story. You have to do all of this, because as an evangelist you are presenting the Church to them. You are a sign of God's work reaching out to them where they are. If you don't listen, and focus too much on your church and on what you have to offer, then you will fail to make the transformative connection. What interests you about the church may not interest the other person.

Make sure, by listening, you are connecting them to the things that they think are important. Ruff says, "A classic trap is doing a really good job in talking about the wrong thing. This means periodically asking and really listening to the response as to whether the topic under discussion is a priority for the customer. If the answer is no—it's time to change topics."[9] The same goes for prospective members. We aren't just listening because we want new members; we are listening because we care about the individual. A generous evangelist is a great listener and knows when to speak and when to be quiet.

The future Church will have many opportunities for an individual to take a first step. Adopting the Episcopal Church as your community, and its gospel of God in Christ Jesus as your gospel, will be life-changing. It need not have barriers so high that no one wants to be or feels that they are worthy to be a part of it. That is not a grace-filled way of going about being Christian community. The future Church and its evangelists will understand that God's mercy, forgiveness, and love is truly free, and there is nothing anyone can do to earn it—not even joining the Episcopal Church.

Evangelists are humble; they love their Church and Jesus but do not put down others. Good evangelists also don't focus only on the people they want to spend time with. They will spend time with anybody who is truly interested. They are eager to help someone try on the Episcopal Church, to renew their faith or find new faith in God. Because the evangelist is humble about their work and their community, there is no reason to lie. Evangelism is not lying or selling a product you don't believe in. Evangelists are honest about their community and how it works. It takes a lot of energy to lie. If you are an evangelist and you have to lie for your community, then you either need to go find a cause and community that better suits you, or you need to stop and help your community sort itself out. Don't be passing along bad stuff to others. I believe we all know what is good and what isn't. Passing along a dead church to a new generation is not our work.

## Discussion Questions

1.  How does one strike a balance between the clarity and humility that generous evangelism calls for? What spiritual practices can we undertake to make space for a "humble clarity" to develop within us?

2.  In this chapter Bishop Doyle offers a brief history of evangelism. What about this history most surprised you? Disappointed you? What important lessons might the future Church learn from Doyle's history of evangelism?

3.  Evangelism is about sharing the gospel. What do you think the "gospel" is? Have you ever shared the gospel with anyone before? What was the experience like?

4.  Bishop Doyle says that generous evangelism will "focus on interested people who are curious about God." Do you agree? Have you ever tried to motivate someone to attend Church or to pursue a relationship with God that just wasn't interested? What was the outcome?

5.  Do you frequently invite people to attend church with you? Why or why not?

112

## Spiritual Exercise

Bishop Doyle says that the generous "evangelist must get beyond insider speak." Think of five "insider words" that are often used in the Episcopal Church and write them down on a piece of paper. Next, write a definition of each word using ordinary, common, non-churchy language. Check your definitions to make sure that you don't use insider language to define your insider terms. Show your definitions to a friend not acquainted with the Episcopal Church and request feedback as to whether or not your definitions make sense. Finally, choose a new and more accessible word that captures the essence of each "insider word" that you defined.

*Suggested Passage for Lectio Divina:* Luke 10:1–9

## Suggested Reading

Susan Snook, *God Gave the Growth: Church Planting in the Episcopal Church.* New York: Morehouse Publishing, 2015.

Caesar Kalinowski, *Small Is Big, Slow Is Fast: Living and Leading Your Family and Community on God's Mission.* Grand Rapids, MI: Zondervan, 2014.

# 10

# The Future of Stewardship

When we glance over the history of the Christian Church, what can we see when we look for telling signs of stewardship? We know that some of the early communities shared everything they had. They lived in community and everything was held in common. We know that they took up collections for the poor, and that special attention was given to widows and orphans.

As the Church grew and became associated with the state, it received money and support from taxes and benefactors. We know from architecture and history that by the fifth century, the church building had an area where deacons could collect and distribute alms and food for the poor. By the seventeenth century, poor boxes were installed, so that the Church could take up a collection as people entered and then disburse the monies to the poor.

It would be another two hundred years before American congregations made the weekly plate offering part of worship. That's right—we have not always had a plate offering. The reason is that congregations did not depend upon voluntary giving by the membership. Most American churches were still established by governmental authorities, like their counterparts in Europe.[1] Congregational churches and Anglican churches alike were established churches supported by the state. The reason was that church was seen as more than just a societal norm; it was seen as a requirement for good citizens. Church was a public good, so taxes and fees were collected from the people to support its work. Even after the American Revolution and the writing of the Establishment Clause of the First Amendment, churches were still by and large supported by the state. This would last until 1833, when Massachusetts revoked the religious tax and every other state soon followed. This changed everything.

Christian communities, for the first time in centuries, had to figure out how they were going to survive without government assistance. This is when pews became rented and paid for by local families. The leadership of the church sold, taxed, and rented pews in order to secure funds for the building and for ministry.

You can see George Washington's family pew at Christ Church in Alexandria, Virginia. He also had one at St. Paul's Chapel in New York City and at Christ Church in Philadelphia.

Eventually the pew rentals went away as congregational leadership found it better to set a budget and invite the parishioners to pledge the funds needed for the year. They would literally pass a book around to the heads of the families and have them write their pledge in the book. By the nineteenth century, many churches had a few churchmen meeting and setting the budget with the priest.

Over time, congregations moved to an annual ingathering of pledges, when parishioners could tell the church how much they intended to give during the following year. Eventually, in the second half of the twentieth century, the tradition of pledge campaigns or stewardship drives was the modus operandi of churches in the United States. Until recently, this was how the Church funded ministry.

The theological bases for stewardship have been as diverse as its practices. Theologically, stewardship has shifted from a call to possess land and give thanks to God, to the Church's right to oversee the governments of the world, to the divine right of kings, to noblesse oblige, and finally, in the last century, arriving at a tithe of 10 percent as the norm for Christian giving. Modern Protestants have made the tithe the theme of their stewardship campaigns. It is worth remembering that the actual passage wherein the biblical tithe is mentioned is not what most people think. The tithe is actually more like 22 percent when you add up the total God requires in Leviticus and Numbers (Lev. 27:30–33, Num. 18:20–21; Deut. 12:17–18; Deut. 14:28–29).[2] Moreover, the tithe is the minimum gift that is to be offered, not the norm or maximum. The requirements of percentage giving and animal sacrifices during the age of the first and second Temple, in the Old Testament, far outnumbered a tithe.

Jesus teaches about stewardship as well. He is clear that the economy that the religious leaders have created is flawed and in need of reform. He says that when the poor give, they give more out of the little that they have, than the rich do when they make a large gift. The poor make a proportionally larger gift.

Jesus offers a particular theology. He tells those who follow him that everything is God's. God is the creator of all things, the maker of all things, and the one who oversees all things. Jesus offers a radical vision of people who are directly in relationship with God because of God's love. He teaches that their care for one another and the community in which they live is essential to the health of their relationship with God. He tells those who will listen that they are to make use of the wealth they have, to multiply it, and to be generous and honest with it. Jesus teaches us that the stewardship question we are supposed to ask is *not* about what to do with all the stuff that God has given us. It isn't my stuff. It isn't your stuff. Instead, Jesus tells us to question ourselves about what we are going to do with all of God's stuff, with God's world, and with God's resources. This was a much more important concept—so important that it is the theme of giving throughout the New Testament epistles and the early Church. The early Church fathers do not mention the biblical tithe.

Making a tithe pledge to support a church is no longer sufficient for Christians navigating the world in which they find themselves. The world is in ecological crisis. Governments fail to provide for the well-being of all their citizens. There is a gulf growing between the rich and the poor. These forces and the anxiety people carry with them about their financial future have shifted the contemporary stewardship conversation. It now focuses upon individuals, their place within their community, their relationships with others, and most of all their relationships with the world around them. Mix these social connections together, and the future of Church stewardship begins to emerge. Stewardship will be for the future Church a discussion dependent upon the health of connection, and its focus will be much broader than support of a building and a priest—it will be about nothing less than transforming the world.

Connection is an essential ingredient to any discussion the future Church will have about stewardship. Scott Bader-Saye believes that affection is the key to this discussion, because people no longer want to simply give money.³ People long to give and receive affection, and this desire to be connected leads them to want to be a meaningful part of the lives of others across the social boundaries of rich and poor. No longer will there be anonymous philanthropy—the point is not just the money but the connection of real people one to another, bound together in bonds of affection, working for the betterment of lives and communities.

The future Church, living Christian communities, will thrive only if they are intimately connected to the communities that surround them. The nonprofits, nongovernmental organizations, and churches that survive in the next twenty to forty years will be entities committed to improving the intrinsic value of their community and those who live therein. To do this, Christian communities will have to have considerable connections with people and their civic context. Christians and their communities will have an accountable and conscientious bond with the world around them. They will have to have affection for the people and communities in which they find themselves.

Christian communities must understand that they do not inhabit a world apart from the world around them. Stewardship conversations of the future will understand that we exist in a particular place, that we belong to it, that we are called to not destroy the things that God has made. Future stewardship will speak about our unique place within the kingdom and our responsibility to be answerable to God about what we did with it. The future Church will have affection for the society and be inextricably connected to it. This will be an ecological, an economic, and a social understanding. As we find our community and are rooted within it, we will also find there neighbors, friends, loved ones, and strangers "with whom we share our place," in the words of Wendell Berry. He writes:

> The word "affection" and the terms of value that cluster around it—love, care, sympathy, mercy, forbearance, respect, reverence—have histories and meanings that raise the issue of worth. We should, as our culture has warned us over and over again, give our affection to things that are true, just, and beautiful.⁴

Whereas in the present we see stewardship conversations that have themes of ecology, economy, social activism, and church finances, in the future we will have conversations about stewardship that help form individuals who understand that everything is connected. The microcosmic conversation about electricity for a building will be understood as being one of global importance. Christian communities who wish to be part of the lives of the new generations of individuals who have grown up in the midst of global economic and ecological crises will treat these themes reverently and with much consideration.

In a lecture given to the Institute for the Future, Jerry Michalski, founder of REX (Relationship Economy eXpedition), offered a vision of how organizations can thrive in a "relationship economy."[5] As a young country, he said, we moved from an agrarian economy to an industrial economy. Now, we have moved most recently to an economy based upon information and knowledge, both of which (like agriculture and industry) have been commercialized. We are growth-addicted and focused upon our national wealth. He recognizes the fragility within this system and the vulnerability it brings.

Michalski believes that the organizations that will thrive in the future will be based in relationships. They will be genuine—rooted in the real and in real people. These organizations will be open to participation by all. They will be free to the user, social in nature, and embody a sense of trust. Here is the biggest takeaway from Michalski's presentation: relationships are not economic, and they are not between an organization and a human being.

The future Church and its Christian communities must grasp the essential stewardship ingredient of the future—stewardship is not about church economy, it is about relationships. Christian community has one purpose and one purpose only, and it is not an economic one. The purpose of Christian community is to connect people to God and to connect people with people. Stewardship is about the health and vitality of the relationships Christians have.

All organizations are trying to figure out the new relationship economy—so they can capitalize upon it. This is not our purpose. Our purpose is to seek to have a conversation about stewardship that helps people connect their giving with their values and to their belief in a God who cares and who helps people connect to one another. Michalski offers organizations some ideas about how to begin this conversation, and his points are worth reflecting here as we think about the future Church.

We must begin by rebuilding trust—relational trust. This kind of trust-building does not bring financial benefits. Trust is rebuilt when the community is the beneficiary and not the church. Leaders will have to choose to make trust and community impact the measurements of health and vitality and not the old economic measurements of pledges and average Sunday attendance. Christian communities of the future will have to be visible to the world around them embracing new partners. Language like "pledging units" will need to evolve. We cannot treat people like inter-changeable units and then expect them to behave like human beings.

What is taking shape globally is a gift economy; this is one of the future artifacts that is present today and is important for our conversation around stewardship. Our goal as a transformative Christian community is to reach huge numbers of people and motivate them for the common good, while decreasing overhead costs and any negative drag on our mission initiatives. Relationships are our currency, and our mission of service is to increase the investment of individuals in the community.

Engaging in stewardship for a new millennium will mean losing some predictability and creating more work around connecting individuals with one another and their causes, using new technologies and new methods as giving platforms. Those wishing to give might be moved by a news event or life event, maybe even in the middle of the night, so opening doors to accessible giving will be essential for future stewardship.

Stewardship conversations in the future will not tell the members what we are doing and then invite them to give to a budget. Instead, they will look for giving partners who understand the mutuality involved in steward-ship. God is looking for partners, and as partners we are to work together for the mutual building up of God's creation and God's community. Future stewardship may include sweat equity and hands-on work. No longer will stewardship be the work of check-writing. The difference will be that the service and hands-on work will be outside of the church building, instead of in service *to* the church. Just as there will be no more anonymous phi-lanthropy, there will also be no toxic charity.[6] Instead people will look to truly improve the lives of their neighbors in cooperation with them.

Healthy stewardship in the future will be transparent about where the funds go and how they are used. It will be evident that the use of the funds is responsible and responsive to the world. Future Church stewardship will not demean or undermine the individuals it seeks to serve but will treat both the donor and the recipient with respect and dignity. I believe that connection is essential in the conversation about stewardship. The church's currency is relationships, and as such it is primed to participate in a world economy shifting from shallow consumerism to transformative, shared lives.

As we look for artifacts in our present time, we can see this change occurring even now. The ability to pledge and set up an electronic monthly payment has leveled out giving and created more predictable budgeting. It means that there is no summer lull when givers are on vacation. Electronic banking is slowly doing away with cash, and services such as the Square allow even small businesses to be mobile. This trend will bring about the end of carrying cash, and we will have to rethink how we deal with the offering plate on Sunday morning. Remember, the offering plate is a relatively new invention. It is okay if it goes away or transforms into something else. Electronic banking will move this process along. Many parishes see electronic banking as an important ingredient in maneuvering into the stewardship of the future. We now have more and more churches with giving kiosks. The temptation will be to see this as the future. Electronic banking is only the first step of technology affecting stewardship.

A kind of disconnect between individual and community comes with electronic banking. Once the giving is set up on a monthly basis, it is unlikely that the individual will change it—either to make it lower or higher. Without continued storytelling and involving the individual and family in the community narrative, it is unlikely to increase. This disconnect can lead a community into a false sense of security. The goal for Christian communities will be to build a constant narrative of involvement with real stories of transformation and multiple opportunities to participate and give throughout the year.

With everyone subjected to a steady stream of competing communication, Christian communities will have to communicate how giving changes lives. The annual campaign will be transformed into yearlong stewardship conversations about real people with real opportunities to make a difference through their giving. We already see this transition with yearlong stewardship calendars being created and posted for sharing.

Year-round stewardship fits with our theology that we are stewards of God 's creation every day and have constant opportunities for giving. However, we can't just tell people to give once a month for twelve months. We need to connect them to ministries and giving opportunities all year. It is good to talk about stewardship, but is better to connect a parishioner with a young person from the community and then have them share their story of mentoring and transformation. Year-round stewardship connections will be made when *theology* and *personal narrative* are amplified by electronic giving tools. Christian communities need to use their communication and connection tools to lead individuals to things that they believe in, understand, and feel to be important. They will respond with their money and time.

The future Church will spend time working with people on projects that they are interested in supporting. By making intimate connections, the future Church will increase its stewardship impact on the community, by creating small giving economies. In the past, large churches have had the most impact. I believe that in the future Church we will see a diversification of communities making even bigger impacts. Not unlike micro industries, small congregations can have a big impact on their local community. In the new stewardship economy, the most important technology is the "technology of social relations," regardless of size.

The Christian community of the future will create social opportunities such as meet-ups. These meet-ups will include a mix of parishioners and nonparishioners working together on a topic or project that impacts the wider community. This is not part of our current stewardship model, but it will be essential in the future. People have to be involved in the organization they are helping to fund. It takes the same amount of time to specialize as it does to generalize. The future Church will understand that specializing in unique opportunities helps to resonate with the charisms of the individual community members and ultimately to drive opportunities to give and have an impact.

There are several ways technology is being used to build economies. The Church can learn from them.

ScholarMatch (http://scholarmatch.org/) was created by David Eggers in 2010. Graduating high-school seniors in need of funding tell their story online, and donors interested in creating scholarship opportunities help pay their tuition. Together, real students in need meet real donors and together make their way through college. As of 2014 ScholarMatch had raised more than $650,000 for students, many of whom are the first to attend college in their families. Imagine linking graduating seniors in a church with this type of tool. Or imagine a collective site called SeminarianMatch where future scholars, priests, and teachers for the church can get help with their training, thanks to people committed to Christian education and the formation of ministers.

Micro venture sites such as LendFriend (lendfriend.com) and GrowVC (group.growvc.com) are services where donors and investors connect online about projects, individuals, and start-ups.[7] The peer-to-peer relationships they facilitate make boundaried and safe investments possible and provide low-interest ways of building an economy.

In 2005, a startup called Kiva (kiva.org) began to help entrepreneurs and small business owners in developing countries get low-interest loans.

Their first project, in Uganda, is today a huge piece of the economy in one of Africa 's most populous countries. In 2009 Kiva began domestic loans in a similar fashion.[8] They are built on personal relationships that begin as simple investments and a desire to help many who currently have no other means of receiving a hand up. Through 2014, Kiva had made possible over 1.2 million loans for more than $660 million.

The future Church will be involved in creating similar structures. We will see congregations, parishioners, and members of the community in which the church makes its home all working to create micro financing and ventures possible. Connecting ministry opportunities with those who are interested will happen on Kiva-style sites. Still others may develop projects linking the larger Christian community and a community project, enabling a broader participation in a local innovation that can change the community. These may be focused on service opportunities like health, clean water, wellness, or micro loans to safely help families in need. Imagine a future Church that is interested in helping improve the financial security and overall well-being of the community. Archbishop of Canterbury Justin Welby's desire to have Church credit unions that outperform payday lending businesses by offering lower interest rates is a good example of one way micro ventures can shape stewardship. Imagine if this micro lending were available online for congregations, connecting those in the community who wish to lend with those who need to borrow.

Service is not the only way that the future Church will use crowd funding. In 2012 the Episcopal Church planted three new churches across its 110 dioceses.[9] This is obviously not adequate to meet the need for new church communities. In the future, a successful Church planting strategy will resemble a funding tool like Kickstarter (www.kickstarter.com), which allows investors to support projects. The growing reluctance to send money to denominational and judicatory offices will require new and innovative ways of funding new Christian communities. Both nondenominational churches and denominational churches will use crowd-funded dollars to start new communities. Some of these will be stand-alone congregations, while some existing congregations will use this method to form satellite congregations.

Diocesan leadership might use crowd funding to start congregations for new immigrant populations, thus increasing participation in building venture capital for new churches. Some of the congregations birthed in the next decades will use shared and public space to meet, participate in nongovernmental service ministries, and use coffee shops for their office hours and Bible studies. Based on the Internet, these communities will use crowd funding to support their mission, in the process raising not only capital but also interest and participation.

The maker movement supported at sites like Kickstarter will be a catalyst for innovative economies and innovative stewardship. The new makers are not selling their ideas to big corporations, so they remain small and focused. The future Church at the local level will approach innovation and creativity in the same way. Localized and adaptive community mission will be made possible when it moves away from thinking it needs to act like the big churches in a denomination, which requires a lot of overhead.

Freeing new Christian communities from the institutional overhead that takes away from mission is a financial necessity in the expensive world of church planting. In the Kickstarter model for future Church planting, money will be available to the new idea as it is needed and not before, increasing financial pliability and decreasing the work of getting upfront capital. To have a healthy and whole Christian community in the maker model means having parishioners and community members who are part of its creation. They are invested. They then become the chief evangelists for the new idea and product. Likewise parishioners and community members will become the chief evangelists for the new Christian community or service ministry. And if it doesn't get adequate funding, it is either the wrong time or the wrong place.

We are not in the business of growing financial returns to maintain a budget. We are in the business of God 's mission. Stewardship is about participating in God's economy—in God's provision for the world where there is enough. It is about using what we have to enlarge God's community. Stewardship is not simply about giving; it is about being involved in creating a new world—a transformed world. Stewardship, with all its networking and crowd-sourcing potential, is about connecting individuals with God and with their neighbor.

In an important book by Clay Shirky entitled *Cognitive Surplus*, he says that since 1940 there has been an exponential increase in free time, as I observed in the discussion of Average Sunday Attendance. There are many more opportunities for us to use our free time today. He would argue that we have more opportunity to be creative and collaborative. The time we have to contribute is growing, and we as individuals are participating across many new portals and in many new projects.[10]

We are, according to Shirky, creating a new era of human expression. Marina Gorbis in her work on the nature of the future says that digital natives are now sharing themselves across a multitude of platforms, giving and sharing ideas and money in a new more socially connected universe. We are doing a lot of this work, this using of our cognitive surplus, without receiving what is essential in modern economies—monetary rewards.[11]

The question for the church is: What kind of surplus do we have that might be networked with this wider global movement? The answer is: the stewardship of our relationships. The living and thriving future Church will participate in this global evolution by using its surplus of connected individuals and communities across the globe and supporting a new stewardship of ideas, money, and support. Future Church stewardship will be the means by which we live out our connection to God and to our neighbor.

## Discussion Questions

1.  What does the word "stewardship" mean to you? What does it mean to say that Christians are called to steward that which belongs to God?
2.  What resources other than money has God given you to steward? How can each resource be used to enhance and strengthen relationships?
3.  Bishop Doyle says that the future Church will emerge only as we rebuild "relational trust." With whom has the Church lost relational trust? How did we lose this trust? What must the Church do to regain trust?
4.  Do you pledge a percentage of your income to support the ministry of the Church? If so, what motivates you to give? In what way does the practice of giving enhance your spiritual life?
5.  How can technology be used to enhance relationships? In what sense can technology diminish relationships? How do you envision the future Church making use of technology for the sake of mission?

## Spiritual Exercise

Using the chart below (or recreating a similar chart yourself), consider how you can use each resource to connect people in a way that promotes human flourishing. As you do this exercise, bear in mind that "your" time, money, gifts, etc. do not belong to you but to God. For each resource listed, write down at least one action you can take to improve what Doyle calls "the intrinsic value" of your community.

| Time | Spiritual Gifts |
|------|-----------------|
|      |                 |
| Money | Creation |
|      |                 |

*Suggested Passage for Lectio Divina:* Matthew 25:14–30

## Suggested Reading

Eric H. F. Law, *Holy Currencies: Six Blessings for Sustainable Missional Ministries.* St. Louis: Chalice Press, 2013.

Charles R. Lane, *Ask, Thank, Tell: Improving Stewardship Ministry in Your Congregation.* Minneapolis: Augsburg Press, 2006.

# 11

# Generous Community

In my role as bishop, I travel to each of the congregations under my care. In my first year, I noticed something interesting about our Episcopal Church. In every place, in every size town, and in every kind of congregation, visitors were in attendance. This meant that on any given Sunday in my Diocese, literally hundreds of new people were choosing to attend one of our Episcopal churches. I began to wonder about this and posed this question to anyone who would listen: "What would happen to our Church if we kept 50 percent, or 25 percent, or even 10 percent of those who actually chose to visit our churches each Sunday?" What would happen is that we would grow. We would share God's love with more people. We would be stronger, healthier members of our communities. We would make the world a better place through a growing community.

In 2009, I was invited to be the speaker at the annual Blandy Lectures at Seminary of the Southwest in Austin. I wanted to talk about how we might do the work of discipleship. By the time I finished the lecture outline, I was convinced that we had to begin with welcoming people.

We, as a community, had to do what I call *front door evangelism* well. I asked for help from my friend and coworker Mary MacGregor, who was then the director of leadership and congregational development for the diocese, and she pointed me toward the Leadership Training Network resources on *The Equipping Church*.[1] Here I saw a process of discipleship that invited people, welcomed them, helped them become members, shared with them a biblical understanding of ministry, and invited them to take their place in the community. I adapted it to Episcopal theology and practice. My presentation was received well, and I was convinced that there was more to this for the Episcopal Church.

The Leadership Network process lacked the theology, liturgy, and language of our Church. It just did not quite fit. So I went back to MacGregor, and we made it a priority to create an Invite-Welcome-Connect process for our diocese and for the Episcopal Church. She in turn went to the one individual who has had the greatest success in creating a welcoming process for an Episcopal church in our diocese, Mary Parmer, a consultant. She, with the help of our staff, is the one who put together the best resource on what it means to be a generous evangelism community. You can find these resources at www.epicenter.org/newcomer.

Front-door evangelism is about meeting Jesus when he comes into our community as a stranger. Revelation 3:20 reads: "Listen! I am standing at the door knocking; hear my voice and open the door!" God in Christ Jesus is at the front door of our churches. Jesus is incarnate in the stranger and the visitor. This is in fact connected to our ministry of service mentioned in our biblical understanding of Matthew 25:40, from chapter 4. How we welcome the stranger at our door is in direct correlation to how we welcome Jesus himself. The Rev. John Newton, on our diocesan staff as canon for lifelong formation, helped frame the theology for Invite-Welcome-Connect. He wrote: "The theology for our front-door evangelism is about providing such a home for Jesus in how we invite, welcome, and connect our newcomers and visitors."[2]

The future Church will engage the work of front-door evangelism and more as part of being a generous community. The living, thriving Episcopal Church of the future believes that God is the one sending us newcomers. The future Church understands that how we welcome and connect with them is a primary way in which we make our witness to the grace and love we have received from God. Newton continues, "Front-door evangelism is rooted in an understanding that God sends us newcomers and that as a community we begin bearing witness to our hope in the Gospel—or don't—the second these newcomers set foot on our property. Front-door evangelism sees all visitors as part of the mission field.

When a front-door evangelist sees a new family or a lonely student or a scared senior entering the sanctuary (or parish hall) for the first time she immediately thinks 'the harvest is plentiful.' Front-door evangelists approach visitors so as to encounter them." The generous community of the future is filled with people engaging in front-door evangelism.

The generous community recognizes that individuals come to us with their own narrative. They are people who have been hurt by other churches. They are people who are busy. They are burdened and sometimes feel lost. They are people who are searching. They are individuals who have courageously decided to step out in faith (literally) and enter the doors of our congregation. Generous communities do more than welcome people—they loudly proclaim that we want you to be part of our community. Generous communities in the Episcopal Church embrace the stranger and help them to find a place. They believe that when we fail to make a home for those without, we are being unfaithful to the God we believe in.

In the Diocese of Texas we say, "As followers of Jesus Christ . . . All are sought and embraced in worship, mission, and ministry in a spirit of mutual love and respect." This is our vision statement.[3] I believe that the future of not just our diocese but the Episcopal Church as a whole will be known as a generous community where *all* are sought and embraced in a spirit of mutual love and respect. The future Church understands that the life of the community is enriched as new members are incorporated.

The future Church will discard the belief that people want to be left alone. How can that be true? Well, the newcomer actually got up early on a day off and intentionally entered a church. People who want to be left alone would not go through all that it takes to get to church. That doesn't make sense. This is simply a lie we tell ourselves, so we are removed from the responsibility of meeting Jesus in the stranger. The future Church will cultivate new practices of invitation, welcome, and connection that are rooted and grounded in the gospel of Jesus Christ building and growing generous communities.

Big or small, the thriving Episcopal community of the future will engage the following evangelism in an innovative, generous, and accountable manner. Many churches fail at their work of evangelism because they work only one part of the generous evangelism equation. They either work on invitation and are unprepared to connect people, or they work on the welcome piece but never invite, or any combination of the essential ingredients. Generous communities must be prepared with an intentional process of linking newcomers into the community. The Church will take this seriously enough to have designated people who will connect and keep track of newcomers. They will be generous listeners and be trained in this ministry. They will help the newcomers understand how God is moving in their lives and aid them in using their particular life journey, gifts, and talents to enrich the community.

The future Church will have clarity about the needs of the community and how individuals can enter deeper community life. These communities have clear boundaries and can articulate and explain the rites of initiation (baptism, confirmation, and reception). Past generations who were raised in institutions knew how to navigate church life, which was at that time less complicated. Individuals today, in a culture where everything can be personalized, have less experience navigating complex community life. Church life tomorrow will have to deal with the integration of community ideals with the individual desire to personalize their experience. This will put pressure on the best of organized communities with the clearest boundaries. It will cause disruption and conflict in Christian communities that do not take seriously the importance of being a self-aware community.

A generous community knows that intentionality is essential to empowering people for ministry. Ways of learning (classes, small groups, and one-on-one) help individuals discover their spiritual gifts and passions. Leaders in the community know that their work is to create disciples. Out of a generous self-giving, they engage newcomers. Ministries are shared and communicated throughout the Christian community so that people know what work the community undertakes. In larger communities, connection is essential, so that individuals can find smaller groups in which to be known and give back. At every level, in every kind of congregation, a generous community evaluates honestly how well it connects the members of the community.

Once a community understands how to do connection, it can work on the tools needed for welcoming. Generous communities know that front-door evangelism will be more effective when first impressions are at their best. The whole experience has to be good. Everything the newcomer experiences will impart a message of generosity and care, or it won't. Today churches are used to communicating only with people they see on Sunday morning. The future Church must communicate far beyond itself, be consistent in its messages, have clean facilities, and install signage that is both visible and understandable. Generous communities will have teams of warm, friendly, and informed people to greet newomers and help them make their way through the service.

Generous communities use diverse leaders of different ages, ethnicities, and languages to welcome people, because they know that God will come to us in many different incarnations. Regardless of size, these communities have clergy who are involved in this work. The clergy and the welcome team intentionally follow up after the newcomer visits for the first time. Then they hold the newcomer's hand as they explore the community. They help the visitor learn more about the community, its purpose, its ministries, and how it makes a difference in the world and in the lives of its members. Simply put, the future Church invites people to meet Jesus and experience the living God in community.

Generous communities know and are known by their neighbors. These communities are good neighbors to the people who live next door. They participate in neighborhood activities and in civic groups and work with their neighbors to create well communities. I have discovered that most congregational leaders today do not know the names of the people who live in the houses or apartments across the street from them. In generous communities, they will be known within the wider neighborhood as essential and helpful citizens. They understand that their impact is dependent upon knowing people and being in relationship.

Generous communities communicate. Clergy and laity alike will be constantly involved in communicating the good news. Generous evangelism takes place between individuals and through social media to be sure, but it is important to cultivate relationships with the local media as well. As civic leaders and good neighbors, clergy and laity will be engaged in communicating to and with their neighbors about life within their Christian community as well as life in the wider neighborhood.

The generous community will have an up-to-date, relevant, and newcomer-friendly website that speaks to the seeker without all the insider language and acronyms. The future Church will engage with newcomers who visit the site. It will invite them to participate in events, share important news, and help them find spiritual resources. Newsletters will be electronic and shared through social media like Facebook, Twitter, or whatever tools are helpful to the community. The future Church will take feedback from Yelp and Google reviews seriously and will encourage visitors and members to use these as a means of giving and receiving feedback. Evangelism in the future Church is connected and entwined with the newest technologies. But it will also have a website either buried below the front-facing one or a separate one for members.

Some Episcopal churches are already engaging in generous community evangelism. We can see the artifacts of the future in these parishes. Technologies are already changing business and how they engage with their clients. You and I are already participating in and using many of them as we buy music, go to dinner, or choose a local cleaner. The future Church will also use these technologies.

The technological age began as a means of manipulating information, with massive room-sized computers doing complicated equations. Humans still had to do a lot of the work in order to get the machine to do what they wanted. Then the Internet became a way that humans could share information. Only a decade ago the Internet was a way to put information out there for people to find. As information became mobile, technology is engrained in our context like never before. The future Church will, like its citizens, be enmeshed in these systems. We as a Church must enter a new mission field—the world of persuasion—an opportunity as real and as vital as the great missionary movements of the past. The Institute for the Future reports, "Our understanding of persuasion, attitude formation, and behavior change is evolving, not only through traditional disciplines like psychology and economics, but increasingly through neuroscience, game design, and the development of new persuasive technologies."[4] There will have to be moral and ethical debates about the use of this technology to be sure. Yet our work here is to think seriously about how the Church will participate.

Part of what is happening is called the creation of our *digital mirrors*. Perhaps you have taken a quiz recently on Facebook, posted something to your blog, tweeted a particular quote you liked, filled out your likes and dislikes, or even forwarded a news article to your friends—this is your digital mirror. Complex programs (algorithms) are able to capture and reflect our digital activity. Opinions we have, how we act, where we go, who we are connected to, and who we are digitally may be collected and seen as a kind of online profile. This might be news to you. Remember all those user agreements you have signed over the years—and not read? Well, guess what? That has given permission to your social networks to mine your information.

If I choose to, I could share my fitness routine (in real time), my list of contacts, my schedule, pictures of my confirmations and parish visits. I am after all a public figure. So, while you might not care how many miles I walked today, the rest of it might be of interest, and as a public figure it might be expected of me to provide this public profile. All of us are creating these digital mirrors of ourselves. It might be fun to figure out what character in the Disney movie *Frozen* I am (I did this last night, and I am Sven the Reindeer), but the greater challenge as with all technology and innovation is to figure out how these algorithms and information can be used to make my life easier—our lives easier. How can my digital information help me navigate the complex world I live in, lose weight, or make my calendar work smoothly? These are more important questions. Self-improvement is one of the fastest growing areas in technology.

One of these new technologies is the Personal Performance Coach created by a group called Accenture Technology Labs. Designed for business and sales, the technology analyzes phone conversations to help individuals share more equally. Remember that listening is important in evangelism. In sales it is essential, and this software will give real-time coaching to the individual on the line and offer accolades for change. What is happening is that technology is being programmed to watch us, record us, and give us feedback on how we can better perform at those things we want to improve.[5] Accenture is focused on self-comparison. One can easily imagine using tools like this to train generous evangelists or assist clergy in preaching performance.

For the competitive among us, many more systems will give feedback based upon other people's performance. TweetPsych, for example, creates a "psychological profile" for individuals based upon their Twitter postings, measuring things like the topic of a tweet and whether it is positive or negative. Results are then given back to the individual, creating a crowd-feedback loop. Humans are likely to deviate or alter performance and conduct based upon what the crowd is doing or thinks about us—we are susceptible to conditioning by our peers. As social creatures, we care what the crowd thinks about us. This technology gives us the opportunity for greater transparency regarding such influences.

These digital mirrors will give us greater opportunity to be self-reflective, and they will enable our technology to be more adapted to our individual lifestyles. The online community changes as we react to different initiatives. That is how all those ads that we actually might be interested in arrive on our Facebook page. I was just recently shopping for some shoes on Google for my wife and later checked my Facebook newsfeed, and up in the right-hand corner was an ad for the same shoes. That is how it works. Google, Facebook, AOL, and all the rest feed us news stories we like and keep stories we might not like from us. All of this is based upon the digital image we create.

Future Church leadership must acknowledge that they and their churches will have digital mirrors and understand their reality, their importance, and their power. The age of persuasion will create digital mirrors for institutions, and Christian communities will have them—good and bad, wanted or unwanted. These technologies are important because people will use them to connect to the church. It is all about the crowd and how we network with others. Moreover, churches and communities that don't take this seriously will be less discoverable within the world where the digital native dwells. I believe that some churches will in fact use digital mirrors to help them connect with interested seekers, leading to new members. The purpose of understanding this is to comprehend how individuals will use these mirrors to participate in the world around them.

The digital native exists in the world with the whole network at their fingertips. In the span of time since 2004 (the birth of Facebook) we have moved from very little contact with other individuals to complete access. This is of course changing everything from business to parenting. Instant messaging (IM) has completely reshaped the art of the conversation. I recently sent a text message to my daughter, on a mountain in Tennessee, from a mountain in Rocky Mountain National Park, with a funny video of her sister. I also sent her money from the same phone from the same location. My car can check my social media and take verbal direction and reply if needed. Like many new cars, it also has Wi-Fi. As a person who "offices" out of my car, I find this can be both helpful and distracting. These are new norms that are shaping our behavior in positive and negative ways. These networks are becoming more and more interactive; indeed, they are proactive. Recently while traveling through London's Heathrow Airport, an app told me that there were friends nearby and invited me to contact them so we could connect. As the Institute for the Future observes, "As devices sense behaviors and environments, they will begin reporting not only to their owners but also directly to online networks."[6]

The future Church must be involved in creating a space within the crowd, a place where people can perhaps track their life of meditation, report on their pilgrimage, keep their spiritual journals, or participate with others in group reflection. If a person wants to make sure they get in twenty minutes of silent time each day, imagine a program that can track the data. The Fitbit strapped on my wrist tracks my exercise and sleep patterns, but it could just as easily track meditation. The Nike+ app helps you measure your activity by GPS. Imagine if you wanted to track your Church participation. Both apps also encourage connections, so that friends can cheer you on. The future Church will use the "crowd on our shoulder" technology as a means by which we might grow in relationship with one another. Individuals will be using these technologies to improve their lives. They will make a natural jump to include their spirituality and time off in these crowd technologies. This will be an important part of the future Church's mission efforts.

Today, everyone knows where everyone else is. Recently my daughter, a new driver, got lost. Using her cell phone and my Apple "find my phone" technology on my iPad at home, we helped her get to her destination via Google maps. It was kind of like being a parental air-traffic controller for my kid. There are, in our phones, on our computers, in our cars, and in our work environments many different sensors that are tracking our location. American Express knows where I am, based upon my spending patterns, and so is better able to protect me from fraud. This is helpful to me, but it is also a way in which they are able to intervene in my life through their network.

There are many emerging technologies for tracking our behavior. My friends have a tool that controls the temperature in their house based upon their movements. My car senses things around it and highlights what it finds for me. Apple has applied for a patent that will enable my iPhone to sense my heartbeat. These telepathic technologies will know where we are and how we are feeling. They will be able to sense who we are and how we are doing and then respond to us.

One of these new programs enables what is called the instant discount. I already get these coupons and incentives to purchase or stop by a favorite coffee shop or restaurant when I am nearby. Yes, Starbucks tells me when I am nearby a coffee break. They do this by using sensors combined with a geo-fence, which identifies my location and invites me in. The future Church will tap into these networks. Today we talk about the importance of a website. Today we rely on people finding our church by location, invitation, or a Google search. I predict that in the future our Church's own geo-fence will communicate with people as they pass by. Based upon their likes and dislikes they will be told what is happening at a church near their location. Imagine a person who is committed to being socially responsible, or interested in helping the homeless, discovering (as they pass by a church) that the church has the same interests. Perhaps the person even receives an invitation to join a Saturday service project.

Just think what happens when you combine the power of geo-location or geo-fences with chosen likes and the ability to know how you feel. Imagine that your phone reads your bio state and then recommends a good Thai restaurant, because you like Thai food and you haven't eaten Thai in while. Microsoft and others are designing software that will "automatically detect frustration or stress in the user" and then "offer and provide assistance accordingly." We will drive cars that know when we are fatigued. We will sit in office chairs that know when we need to move.[7] All of this programming aims to help us manage the world around us.

Imagine then the same users creating spiritual interfaces. In a world of constant stimulation and communication, spiritual seekers may choose to have their technology find for them places of peace and quiet, places of retreat, and places with groups interested in religion or spiritual practices. Imagine a phone app telling you that you are overly stressed and that St. Swithin's in the Swamp has a yoga class at 6:30 followed by a healthy meal. It is around the corner. No charge. Then it includes a list of other neighbors attending, perhaps even a few you know. Imagine an app that notices you have had a busy day of errands and that St. Julius has a meditation class this afternoon or a speaker on a better organized life on Saturday. You are free both of these time slots. Then it asks, "Would you like for me to schedule Saturday for you? Your schedule is open." Users are going to be looking for telepathic technology to help them, and the future Church will understand that this technology is a way in which it can spread the news of mission. Using digital mirrors, geo-fences, and other technology, the Christian community engaged in generous evangelism will see these opportunities as ways to connect with people in real time and offer a bit of grace and peace in an overscheduled world.

In these ways, the future Church will be engaged in generous evangelism. It engages intentionally in being a generous community using all tools at its disposal for its work. The future Church is interested and engaged with the digital native, because it understands this is its context. Most of all, the generous community of Christ is engaged, because it desires to be a transformational part of a culture enmeshed with the digital world. The future Church believes and shares the gospel of God in Christ Jesus as an essential building block to well communities and does this through a network found in the digital universe.

Generous evangelism empowers people to act, and builds the individual's capacity for deeper spiritual connection with God and others by becoming a full participating member of the cloud and the crowd. Not everyone is called to be an evangelist, but a thriving future Church will have many evangelists—each in their own way sharing the good news of the Episcopal Church and God in Jesus Christ through their participation as digital natives in the connected crowd.

## Discussion Questions

1.  What is the relationship between discipleship and the practice of intentionally welcoming newcomers? What does the phrase "front-door evangelism" mean to you?
2.  Bishop Doyle says that our default assumption that newcomers want to be left alone "is a lie that we tell ourselves so we are removed from the responsibility of meeting Jesus in the stranger." Do you agree? Why or why not?
3.  What is your congregation's practice of welcoming newcomers? What works well about their current practice? How can their practice of welcome be improved?
4.  How might technology be used to increase our capacity to invite, welcome, and connect newcomers? What are the limitations of technology with respect to newcomer ministry?
5.  Have you ever felt like a "newcomer" before, whether at your church or in some other community? What was your experience of "welcome" like? How has your experience of being the newcomer changed the way you relate to newcomers at church?

## Spiritual Exercise

Bishop Doyle says that "the generous community recognizes that individuals come to us with their own narrative." Go online and watch Chick-fil-A's "Every Life Has a Story" video (https://www.youtube.com/watch?v=hdUH7bS3IxA). How might this video speak to the church's task of generously welcoming newcomers?

*Suggested Passage for Lectio Divina:* Hebrews 13:1–6

## Suggested Reading

Michael Harvey and Rebecca Paveley, *Unlocking the Growth: You'll Be Amazed at Your Church's Potential.* Oxford, UK: Monarch Books, 2012.

Stephanie Spellers, *Radical Welcome: Embracing God, the Other, and the Spirit of Transformation.* New York: Church Publishing, 2006.

# 12

........................................................................................

# Self-Forming Creative Christians

I wonder how you became a Christian? And, what kind of Christian are you? Regardless of the answer, your story and pilgrimage to this point is unique. I was visiting with a friend of mine the other day, and she described a conversation with her fifteen-year-old daughter. The daughter was talking about her interest in Christianity and asking her mother why she did this or didn't do that. Her mom had her own set of questions. In the end she imparted a bit of wisdom: "I have made my journey, this is your journey, kid." Our journey, finding our way, is uniquely ours. It is our journey to make and to direct. The very fact of you and your story speaks to the great diverse creative power that is at work in the cosmos around us. Yet somehow we in the Church have gotten things a little mixed up. We have, along the way, begun to think a dangerous thought. That thought is: the Church makes the Christian. And, in order for the organization of the Church to make such a thing, it must manufacture it like any other great industrial machine.

The age of the machine and of the cookie-cutter Christian is over, except the Church hasn't figured that out yet. It wasn't much of a reality anyway. In order to be the future Church, we must realize the world is filled with self-learners, storytellers, and people making their self-directed way. Today we are moving into a new creative era where we remember an ancient truth—God is weaving a beautiful tapestry of stories in and among us. We are the strands, the stories that God has made. It is the living of that story and the sharing of that story that is vital to a living future Church.

Our story is a story of creativity. We are human beings. We are about being in the world and (according to our Scriptures) about being collaborators with God in the great cosmic experiment of creation. We are co-creators with God. As the great Episcopal educator Verna Dozier once said, we are made to be partners with God. It is about story, and our response to story, and our writing of the never ending story. Dozier wrote, "The biblical story is always to be prefaced by, 'This is how the faith community that produced the record saw it.' It is never to be absolutized as 'This is the way it was.' The story always points the way to an understanding of God that is greater than the facts themselves. I think any understanding of the biblical story that fails to see it as a human response only pointing to the dream of God is itself idolatry."[1]

John Newton, canon for lifelong formation in the Diocese of Texas, writes in his book *New Clothes*, "Scripture is the only narrative that we can immerse ourselves in where, after a while, we hear God say, 'You take the pen for a while.' Although creation and redemption are both finished in God's mind, in a mystical way, as we enter the story, we soon discover that we are characters and have been assigned a leading role! We come to know ourselves as co-laborers with God."[2] All of us have a part. We have a chapter to write. We have a strand to weave with God. Rooted deep in every story is God's reconciling love. That is what we believe together. As Episcopalians, we have a unique way of telling that story as a community woven together.

However, instead of helping individuals find their story, too often we get serious about formation only when a person declares they want to be ordained. Think of the difference between the ancient pattern of baptismal preparation in the fourth century and the contemporary pattern of ordination preparation. It used to be that people would declare to a mentor their desire to follow Jesus and then enter a time of apprenticeship. Today the process of serious Christianity begins when you tell your priest that you believe you are called to ordained ministry. It used to be that you would then be introduced to the community as a neophyte. Now, you are introduced to the Commission on Ministry and then sent to seminary. In the last weeks of seminary formation, you are tested and selected for ordination. It used to be that there was an intensity in the last weeks of Lent as you approached your baptismal day—the day when you and the community became one. Any new priest can tell you their well-rehearsed spiritual autobiography by the time they do their first Eucharist, while many individuals within the church feel disempowered or think their story is not relevant. Some will say that this shift in process is about a growing focus on the clergy that dates back to the Scholastic movement. "Maybe," I say. More than likely, it is just that we are ill prepared for the new culture around us and that we continue to use a model of formation that no longer works in our context.

We see great sweeps of practice back and forth across the millennia of Christian formation. But at its heart is the tradition of engaging individuals. We are story-centered. We tell the story of Jesus and tell people how Jesus and God are part of their story. And we let them ask questions. Questions and answers are vital to helping people learn about the story of God and the story of those who believe in God. This Q&A format has been part of our tradition in a variety of ways. For example, in the story of Philip and the Ethiopian eunuch in Acts, we find that the eunuch's direct questioning of Philip led to his baptism. Inquiry and instruction went together in the early church, with a master and apprentice or a mentor and a student. And, while this was the model for the most part in the Reformation period, we also know that the reformers felt as though with prayer, Bible, and a catechism, a person could begin a journey of self-discovery. It will take all of these methods to navigate the nature of formation in our present context.

Figuring out how we are going to approach formation in the future is essential for us and for our society. In order for the future Church to flourish it must have many varieties of formation—countless strategies. The future Church will enjoy freedom to experiment because it understands that our mission of formation is *stronger* through diversity, adaptation, and variety. The future Episcopal Church will be known as a network of Christian communities that innovates and has many ways people may discover God and their life with God. It will be a Church known as one that engages in storytelling, and its members are invested in new discoveries about one another and those who choose to follow Jesus with them. The future Church will understand that each Christian community, and each participant within that community, is engaging in the work of formation by self-directing their journey through a variety of forms.

Formation practices in the future will chiefly be about enabling individuals to see that the miracle of life that is in fact present in their being is the same miraculous force that is at work throughout all creation. The power of God that formed the cosmos, shaped galaxies, made heavens and earth, and has given breath to every creature under the heavens is the same force that is at work in their own body, mind, and spirit. Formation in the future Church will be about connecting experiences with conversations.

Perhaps you will say that this is the work of all Christians, and perhaps you are correct. But we also need to recognize that our particular story is an important one in the life of society. The Church, after all, is intended to be a vessel of God's love and mercy to the world. Abandoning the work of forming individuals with a capacity to serve and work for peace has, in many places, left our people adrift. The future Church understands that within the wider global community, it has a voice and a story to tell. It both learns from listening to other stories and offers opportunity for our story to be told. In doing so, we as the future Church participate not only in forming followers of Jesus, but also in forming a healthy civil society. How we form and whom we are forming makes a real-world difference; the future Church must understand this as part of its mission.

The future Episcopal Church will engage in creative formation through a diversity of practices that will take us into a future we can't yet grasp today. Imagine for a moment: the babies we are baptizing in our churches the year I am writing this (2015) will retire in the year 2080. They will enter the workplace in the year 2035, give or take a couple of years. That is the world we are preparing these Christians to enter. The work of Christian formation has never been only about introducing people to God through Jesus Christ. It has forever and always been about helping people find their way to baptism and then to help them figure out how to live life. It is about helping them live a life as a believer in the creative God, the reconciling Son, and the loving Holy Spirit. Everyone, children and adults, has a remarkable capacity for life. Living the creative life is an essential part of formation for the future Church. In order to do this we are going to have to engage in a variety of formation activities. We have to be willing to try things, accept that some things will go wrong, and always be open to trying something else.

Ken Robinson tells a story about a nativity play his four-year-old son was in. He had the part of Joseph. Three boys with towels around their heads walked in as the three kings. They presented their gifts to Joseph, and the first boy said, "I bring you gold." The second boy said, "I bring you myrrh." And the third boy said, "Frank sent this." Everyone howled, of course. But the kids just moved right along. Afterwards, Robinson went up to the little boy and asked, "Are you OK?" and the boy said, "Yeah, why, was that wrong?" Robinson's point is that children, when they start out, aren't afraid of getting things wrong. They grow into it.[3]

We have been running our churches with anxiety that we might get it wrong. Our formation practices have in fact echoed this reality. At our worst we have been trying to convince people of a story about a creative, reconciling, and loving God through a process of formation that saps the creativity out of the seeker. We dampen the spark of questioning, inspiration, and longing for the divine. We have undermined the story we are trying to tell. They are looking for mystery, and we are in many cases offering facts.

Our formation practices came out of the industrial age. They are intimately tied to education practices, which have had similar and parallel development over the past two hundred years or so. The goal, like that of public education, was to produce good members of the industrialized age. Learn things that you need to learn in order to get a job is education's goal, according to Robinson. For the Church it has been the notion that you learned what you needed to know—which is not much—unless you are going to be a monk, priest, or professional religious worker. We are a faith that is dependent upon the sharing of the story with one another. We have often failed to pass along our story to our own.

The future Church must adopt a new way of thinking about formation. It will engage in opportunities for individuals of every age to play and experiment with Christianity and their story, as it relates to the Episcopal way of life. It will reclaim the virtuosity of sharing story visually in art, icons, and images. It will reclaim the art of storytelling through sound, continuing our tradition of hymnody but with all kinds of music, along with speaking and poetry. It will engage movement, pilgrimage, work, play, and dance in all of their myriad forms, because it knows that people learn kinesthetically.[4] It will reinvigorate the art of formation as a multisensory participatory experience where individuals are self-learners who direct their own explorations. This will mean that Christian communities will actually re-create the way in which they think about, integrate, and share story through formative experiences.

I believe that some of our difficulty in doing the ministry of forma-tion is that, like the educational systems around us, we have not believed that people can learn on their own. Instead, we have played out, system-atically, a notion that the work of the Church is to educate people. We are the authority, the power managers, the intermediaries between God and humanity. Therefore, we are the ones responsible for imparting knowledge to others. We have done this blind to the fact that our story from creation forward is about a God who wants to walk in the garden of creation with his creatures.

We have a God who requires no middleman. We have a story that tells us that God is interested in communicating with humanity directly. We have a story that says God comes into the world in the person of Jesus and speaks directly to us and invites us to participate in the re-creation of a peaceable kingdom. This God says, "Come and follow me." Our God is interested in our taking a journey with God, and at the end of days sit-ting at table with us and sharing our stories. Nevertheless, the church has insisted upon a transactional model of instruction for over a thousand years. That transaction model looks like this: *person enters church + class-room introduction + baptism + Confirmation + adult classes (maybe) = Christian.* This is a model that worked when the world was Christian. The models we need to look at are the ones used in the time when Christianity was the minority.

Human beings are created by God to be self-learners. It is our nature. It is the part of us most deeply connected to our instinct. We are created to be curious cocreators and to try new things. Today, as I write this, we know that most people are choosing to visit an Episcopal church because they looked at its website. If you know nothing about a school, business, or restaurant, you look on the Internet. More than once I have gone to a restaurant website to see what people are wearing so I know what is appropriate to wear. The same is true for people looking at churches.

Here are just a few sites that are listed if a person types, "What does the Episcopal Church believe" into the search engine. First you might get our EpiscopalChurch.org site. Second, you might get an article on Wikipedia. Then you might get one that says the Episcopal Church is straight out of the pit of hell. Searching the web is a primary way in which self-learners are looking for what the Episcopal Church believes, and this is their first formative contact with our belief system and people's opinions of it.

The Church has moved into a knowledge economy where exchange and conversation are valued over data, logistics, and organizational practices. Becoming a better machine churning out general Christians will not be the way of the future Church. That Church will be fully invested in forming creative Christians. It will no longer be focused on building efficiencies, systems, programs, and methodologies—instead it will be focused upon innovative processes and how they connect people, on any and every tool that will put the power of connection and discovery directly into the hands of the self-learner.

The Institute for the Future states that "traditional knowledge chains controlled by gatekeeper institutions and organizations, such as publishers or universities, will give way to knowledge ecologies controlled by no one in particular but with access for all."[5] In the past the Church has functioned more like a gatekeeper trying to control access to its life and community instead of being characterized as an organization with a story of sharing wisdom within an ecosystem of accessibility for the self-learner.

The future Church will be prepared for the self-learner and understands the kind of community that they wish to engage. It knows the seeker is even now at the door and looking to see who we are and what we are about. It is invested in its story of creativity and is adept at sharing it. The future Church must out-communicate the narrative of meaningless consumerism by building communities of storytellers who themselves are exploring and learning as they live. It recognizes that it has a multitude of ways in which it can help self-learners find formation and transformation, and it uses them all to build a creative faithful body of Christians who are living together in a socially networked community. So what are the characteristics of the new self-learner and what is their community habitat like?

## Techno Learners and Their Habitat

In 1945, Vannevar Bush was President Roosevelt's science advisor. He was the mastermind behind the Manhattan Project among other things. He wrote an article that year for *The Atlantic* magazine entitled "As We May Think."[6] In the article, he outlined the idea of a device in which "an individual stores all his books, records, and communications, and which is mechanized so that it may be consulted with exceeding speed and flexibility. It is an enlarged intimate supplement to his memory." He called it the "memex." I call it my iPhone. Bush's notion would influence the creation of the Internet, the PC, and much of the way in which we navigate our global stores of knowledge today.[7] Today Bush's idea of knowledge access, storage, and sharing is a reality. When I told a friend that I was working on this book, he handed me John Naisbitt's bestselling book *Megatrends*, published in 1982. Naisbitt pronounced: "We are moving from the specialist who is soon obsolete to the generalist who can adapt." He continued, "In the computer age we are dealing with conceptual space connected by electronic, rather than physical space connected by the motorcar."[8] Remember, that is the year the desktop computer appeared on the cover of *Time*. Today we know that this new ecosystem is where self-learners live.

George Mason University professor of public policy Christopher Hill believes we are on the edge of a creative revolution he calls post-scientific society: "a society in which cutting edge success depends not on specialization, but on integration—on synthesis, design, creativity, and imagination."[9] In a self-learning world, the Church will be integrated with knowledge tools that help it do its work of formation. As mobile devices get more powerful and interface technologies get more sophisticated, interaction within Christian communities will become "always communicating, always forming."

Ross Mayfield, CEO of Socialtext Incorporated, an enterprise social software company based in Palo Alto, California, and leader in information-sharing, says it this way: "NetGens (Net Generation) think of the computer as a door, not a box."[10] The future Church will not be limited to access only when it gathers—it will be forming people throughout its network whenever and wherever the self-learner taps into the community. It will exist in a world where sharing is more "intimate, more oblique, and more immediate."[11] Formation will tap into the lives of individuals, crowds, and groups to create conversations and to connect and convene. It will use online tools—current examples would be Google, Flickr, Twitter, blogs, meetups, and feeds—to share its who, what, where, when, and why. These "tools," in fact, will no longer be just communication equipment but space where formation is happening.[12]

The future Episcopal Church will be populated by amplified humans who are extreme self-learners, accustomed to trailblazing new learning landscapes and applying creativity to sort out their terrain.[13] Whereas their predecessors were interested in getting it correct, making a good exam score, and having the right degree, these extreme self-learners find that the creative process is the product. It is in the learning and the sharing that life happens. These self-learners understand their place in a large web of relationships, and they are consistently probing, learning, discovering, and creating new nodes and forms of faith. They are empowered by technology and have mixed their faith into their life and lifestyle. Knowing that formation is constantly about being aware, they are creating new places for their faith to go, new conversations for it to enter, and new venues in which they can tell their story.

The importance of knowing who we are as Episcopalians and sharing that through a variety of settings now becomes clear. Extreme learners direct their own education, formation, and learning. They automatically share what they are learning and experiencing. For them there is no one classroom with one teacher and a group of students. Everything is a classroom experience and everywhere is the teacher. If you want to learn about the history of education, go find it. How about the story of how the church has been involved in social change—here it is, learn it, and share it.

The extreme learner redefines libraries, classrooms, labs, and the teacher-student relationship. Therefore, the extreme learner within the Christian faith setting will in the future have redefined the role of apostle, catechist, youth director, priest, deacon, parent, and Sunday school teacher. Just as they are designing their own curricula and online courses in universities today, extreme self-learners will rethink and re-create the process by which they become Christians. The future Church, knowing this, makes the creation of an introductory class on Christianity and its practices part of the process of becoming a Christian. The future Church does this because the self-learner is active in the learning exchange and is in fact helping others to learn as they share and make their pilgrimage. They are hacking what is today a closed formation process and sharing it freely into their own networks. They are teachers themselves as they make their way through the information.

The self-learners are on a pilgrimage with God and with any Church that will help them network and gain access to the Holy. They are interested in being like Abram and Sarai—journeying out from their own land of Ur. They want to discover their own path with God, and extreme learners must know the future Church is there to help. They also want to connect—inside and outside the community. With a little guidance and direction they, with the aid of the future Church community, will spread the Good News by sharing what they are in the process of learning.

Extreme learners want to connect with other extreme learners. They meet, make, and choose their own community of mentors. Mentors used to be chosen for you. Tomorrow's church will be engaged in making a network of potential mentors available, allowing individuals to choose multiple mentors for the varied tasks and learning challenges before them. Just as extreme learners are shaping their own formation path, so too, they will select different mentors for the varied legs of the journey.

Extreme learners ask a lot of questions. They do this to challenge and to understand. They also do this for the benefit of others, so that others may understand. They listen carefully and are constantly processing. They are eager and they will make mistakes and say odd things as they are putting the pieces of the formation puzzle together. This will drive present-day Christians crazy and test the community's tolerance. The Church understands that this is part of the formation pilgrimage. Learning fast and failing fast helps the pupil to learn. This is how apprenticeships work, and the future Church must be willing and able to tolerate the extreme learner's eagerness.

The future Church will be ready for this learning revolution. Not unlike every present-day institution, the future Church will have to figure out how to resolve the issues created by extreme self-learners and an old system of hierarchical knowledge transactions. The future Church will make the leap, because its story is one of creativity and innovation; its God is a God of creation. It believes in a God who is constantly muddling around in chaos and inviting transformation out of the whirlwind. It understands that it has the responsibility to take a step into this new culture of creativity and be part of building the "collective future."[14]

The future Church will be a creator of networks of self-learners, artisans, writers, poets, businessmen and women, scientists, and religious leaders collaborating for the health of the community. This will be a new commons. Its formation practices are not oppressive or a colonizing of the mind. Instead, it will serve as a living communal faith lab that leverages vital resources and is flexible, accessible, and adaptive. The Christian community will dwell within a whole ecosystem of learning as an active and contributing influence within the wider network/community of self-learners.

The future Church will invest itself in the production of meaningful materials for the self-learner to access, with spirituality, formation, and vocational discovery resources made available through a variety of platforms and networks. Theologians, professors, spiritual leaders, monks, catechists, and mentors are essential ingredients in these networks. No longer is formation limited to the one priest–one church model. Its liturgy, preaching, and sacramental life will be shared and available anytime and anywhere. It wasn't long ago we laughed at the idea that people might have tablets with the liturgy on it. Today I don't go to a Bible study or worship service where someone isn't accessing the Bible or other texts via their smart device. The future Church will open-source everything and create a flourishing formation ecosystem of two millennia of spiritual teaching, sacred texts, and wisdom writing for the theologically interested. This information will be a rich complement to an environment filled with real-life mentors.

Learning, however, even for extreme self-learners with access to so much wisdom, is still a social undertaking. Learning is relationship-based, and it is the relationship that is the driver in the education process. Marina Gorbis writes, in *The Nature of the Future*, "Many proponents of distance learning miss the importance of relationships and social connections in education. I believe online learning and resources alone will not provide a solution to our educational needs. One needs mentors, someone to look up to and to guide the learning process, to help filter what one needs to know and to provide feedback."[15] It is within the community that ideas are shed, shared, and created. It is in the communal atmosphere that the "desire to learn" is inflamed. With the aid of friends and chosen mentors, the self-learner is able to access and benefit from the "rich ecology of content" we have been talking about. Into this rich ecosystem we must add formation leaders for the future Church.

Leaders in formation will be of varying types given the complexity of the learning environment.[16] Here are a few possibilities:

- *Learning partners* are self-learners themselves who know the key individuals within the community help others to navigate the terrain.
- *Personal advisors* are trained and selected to help individuals create their own formation environment.
- *Wellness guides* will help individuals or a group move to a healthier lifestyle as part of Christian formation.

- *Edu-vators* will help build the technological "platforms," explore innovations, and keep formation accessible across the community.
- *Formation cartographers* will map the external community context and help the Church have access to the collective networks in the community.
- *Social capital designers and developers* will plan and create strategies for people to discover, share, and create resources through collaborative processes.
- *Learning journey mentors* will help connect self-learners with everyone to create unique formation.
- *Formation curators* will help tell the stories of those in the formation process, broadening their impact beyond any one individual's experience.

These are the names of the future formation team members. Regardless of what you call the team members in any given community, or how many of them are full-time employees (which I don't imagine will be many), the future Episcopal Church will need these people. Some churches will have all of these people. More than likely they will be shared regionally. Today in the Diocese of Texas there are three churches of different sizes sharing a social networking person, who does some of this work across the city of Austin.

The future Church, if it is to thrive, must be untethered from a Sunday-only formation process. It is so much more than learning Bible stories. It is not about sitting at the feet of professionals. Formation in the future Church will be about individuals joining together to enjoy the pilgrimage of discovering how the story of God is entwined with our own. Every member of the Christian community of the future is a learner, regardless of age or tenure in the community, and everyone is learning from everyone. In the future Church, formation will move far beyond discipleship. Jesus called disciples, that is true. But no disciple stayed a disciple forever—they became apostles and were sent out.

The gap is closed between apprentice and master in the future Church, because the identity of teacher and student is merged in the self-learning pilgrim. I believe that the potential for socially structured formation brings us back to the vision that Jesus had for the community of God. He envisioned a community of self-learners who were engaged in the work of formation for themselves and others. He envisioned a community making its journey with God and in so doing being remade as a new community of transformation.[17]

## Discussion Questions

1. Bishop Doyle argues that the common notion that "the Church makes the Christian" is a dangerous and outdated idea. What do you think he means by that? Do you agree?
2. What does the word "formation" mean to you? What does a person look like when he or she is formed well? How does formation "happen"?
3. Bishop Doyle says that "living the creative life is an essential part of formation for the future Church." How does one live the creative life? Why is the creative life important? What is the alternative to living the creative life?
4. If not to serve as middleman or to impart divine knowledge, what *is* the local congregation's chief task with respect to Christian formation? How do congregations foster self-learning?
5. Do you consider yourself to be a "self-learning pilgrim"? Why or why not? How has the Church supported (or not supported) your self-learning journey?

## Spiritual Exercise

Go to www.google.com and type "free spiritual gifts inventory" in the search box. After scanning the results, choose a spiritual gifts inventory that best suits you. After getting the results, develop your own self-learning formation strategy to develop and grow in your unique spiritual gifts. You may be tempted to rely on others to craft such a plan for you, but be mindful of Bishop Doyle's thesis: In the future Church there will be no distinction between apprentice and master, but only "the self-learning pilgrim."

*Suggested Passage for Lectio Divina:* Matthew 4:18–22

150

## Suggested Reading

John Newton, *New Clothes: Putting on Christ and Finding Ourselves.* New York: Morehouse Publishing, 2014.

Jim Herrington, R. Robert Creech, and Trisha Taylor, *The Leader's Journey: Accepting the Call to Personal and Congregational Transformation.* San Francisco: Jossey-Bass, 2003.

# 13

..............................................................................................................

# Making Change

So, how will this all happen? What are the ways in which we go about making these changes? How do we lead into the future now that we have some ideas about its potential and possibility? There have been two important leadership moments in my life when a friend and coach has looked at me and said, "You are a leader and you will do it. It is what we need from you." The reality is that we will make our own future—or not. It is up to us to step into our role as citizens of the Church and make this future happen.

In the mechanical world, change is based on solving problems: you find a problem and you come up with a solution. Then, you implement the solution. When that doesn't work you figure out why and you either fix it again or abandon the project. What I have learned, though, is that we really have a limited idea of why things work or don't work. We have a limited view of all the interconnecting parts. We have a norm, a mean, which we perform above or below, but seem to hover around no matter what we do. We redo vision statements, we set new goals, we assign more hierarchies, and build new programs to fix things. But the fixing isn't coming, and we are running out of people to blame. Margaret Wheatley points out that this is not the way that *life* works.[1]

Wheatley offers us a different model that we can apply to life in the organism of the Church. The model goes something like this: Some portion of our community, our organization, experiences *something* that is wrong. The small group decides that this *something* needs attention. They need to learn more about this *something*, so the individuals gather up all the information about it they can—good, bad, and indifferent—and circulate it throughout the network of relationships it has. Other individuals grab on to it and have the same reaction. They amplify it by sharing it. The information is itself changing at this point. It is being interpreted. It is growing. The group (which is larger now) understands it better, and it has more meaning than it did.

The relationship of the disturbance with the overarching organization will become more understandable, and the Church as a whole must deal with the disturbance. It is forced by the meaningfulness of the information, and it is willing and able to let go of a previous understanding of how the organization's experience of the world was ordered. It is able to rethink or change structure, habits, and systems. Yes, this does create some confusion and some chaos. Wheatley says this part is always the most uncomfortable and the most painful. She writes that it is a "state that always feels terrible." So let us be disturbed!

It is in this moment that the future Church becomes apparent. As the old is passing away, the new becomes more visible. The future Church then lets go of the present past and steps into a new way of doing things. This is messy, to be sure. But the future Church operates on process and adaptation, and it begins to reorganize using all the new information about the disturbance. Like a ghost in the machine, the Holy Spirit continues to work and moves within the church, making it new even as the old passes away. The future Church continues to change and make its way into new habits, new ways of governing, and new ways of doing mission. The future Church is different because it understands the world and the world's disturbances differently. The future Church and its citizens understand something now that every other living system understands and lives by, and that truth is that it changes because that is the only way to preserve itself. This is what the ancient Church has always done, and it is what the Church must do as it makes its way into the future. The future Church is even now acclimatizing to the new cultural ecosystem and reproducing and replicating the living parts that will survive the present past Church.

In order to do this, the Church will have to exhibit several essential behaviors as a community. The future Church, as an organism, must find within itself individual members who share the belief in a living Church. They will believe that the mission of God in Christ Jesus is more important than existing power structures and our place in them today. It will not be a failure if some of our current citizens do not participate in the future Church. It will be because they are tied to the present past Church, and they do not hold the ultimate mission as the highest mission. This is natural. They will, however, continue to believe that other disturbances are of more importance. In close examination, shared information that is representative and widely distributed will reveal that the disturbance they are experiencing is a disturbance for a Church organism that no longer exists.

The future Church will network and organize itself into a wide conversation, both to gather information and to share it. "Life," Wheatley says, "insists on participation."[2] There are no shortcuts. As a bishop, I have learned the hard way that no matter how much easier I think it would be if people would just do what I want them to do, this shortcut is never actually a shortcut. I have come to understand that what Wheatley says is true—people want to participate. The work of the future Church and its leadership is to create broad-based networking, communication, and gatherings that enable participatory leadership. What I know about life in the diocese and with her people is that they never obey—they only and always react. What the future Church is interested in is "loyalty, intelligence, and responsiveness."[3] To have those qualities in the life of the future Church, the leadership must share information and focus attention on common work. This is how it will deal with the disturbances it experiences.

The leadership of the future Church knows that its citizens are constantly interpreting their own reality and experience. Wheatley tells us that different parts of all living organisms may experience different sensations or different realities. The organism does not normally lack an idea of what it needs to do but instead unifies around a common response. The future Church will do the same. Just as there is value in the organism of the future Church for sharing our stories, there is value in acting and working together. When the future Church works together it will be able to build commons and amplify its local missions despite the diverse experiences everyone is having. The focus on mission helps continue an organizational life that values individuals who have a different story than the majority of the community. All are valued, all are part, all are enabled to help do the work of God in Christ Jesus. Lastly, the future Church

must connect, connect, connect. The work of connection is so essential because it amplifies the story, it amplifies the work, it amplifies the
essential ingredient of what it means to be Church—connecting to God
and one another. The future Church will thrive in its new environment,
because it has absorbed the idea of working with people's own tendency to
self-learn and self-govern.

One of the ways that we are going to get from here to there is by navigating the future with attention to the areas of change we have already
discussed. This means that the present church will begin to make changes
that integrate the amplified human into the overall structure and ministry of the church. The present Church will explore and then amplify
how current tools are already doing this. What are the ways in which we
are already making connections with people, and how do we create and
enhance what is already working, while at the same time creating new
ways of integrating life in and outside the church?[4]

Another way that the present Church will take a step into the future
is by continuing to focus on the local and supporting the work that is
taking shape there. The broader Church organism must be attentive to
and support the local members in their work to establish mission. Any
time the wider Church structures pull away from this focus on the local, it
disenfranchises the efforts that are having the greatest cumulative effect
on transforming the community.[5]

The present Church will need to begin to use "digital mirrors" to
reflect on itself and its current place within the broader cultural narrative. It will do this in order to better understand where it can position
itself within the broader mission environment so that seekers can more
easily find it. Where is it that the Episcopal Church has an opportunity,
by being itself, to impact and affect local community dialogue in a positive and transformative way? We have to do this in a way that decreases
the walls currently existing between perspective members and existing
communities.

We will need to figure out how to hold one another accountable to
the work that is before us. We are coming out of an age where we measure
everything. "You can't manage what you can't measure," said the statis-
tician and popular engineer Edwards Deming. Number-crunching is the
venue of managers, and we have used them to try to figure out what is
happening in the present Church. The problem is that we are only measuring things we think we see. We then make conclusions about what we
see and we create stories, which become narrative biases.

Wheatley raises a good question we ought to ask ourselves whenever we get into a room and start going over the numbers: "What are the problems in organizations for which we assume measures are the solution? If you agree that these are the general behaviors you're seeking, ask whether, in your experience, you've been able to find measures that sustain these important behaviors over time?"[6] The future Church will invest in receiving feedback from throughout its networks of relationships. It will understand that each context is different and that feedback from any particular place is self-determined. The future Church will value what the local church values and relish the experiences (no matter how small or how great) that are new, surprising, and essential to life and vitality. The future Church will value adaptability, innovation, and wellness rather than stability and control. It must understand that in a VUCA world strength is gained by engaging in the context outside the church community, and to do so is going to create action and reaction, which in turn will build a better, more sustainable community.

The future Church will be looking for revelation throughout its communities. It knows that revelation is deeply connected to the Incarnation and the people of God. Revelation is found in creation and cocreation. Revelation is found in gardening and harvesting. Revelation is found in sharing stories with one another. The future Church values those opportunities and experiences where revelation has potential and will shy away from stable, controlled, and static meaning.

Let me say here a word about the pastoral work that is before us. Clayton M. Christensen came up with a descriptive phrase to help leaders understand how they are supposed to act when doing the thing that brought success in the past is now the wrong thing to do in a new business climate: "the innovator's dilemma." The solution he offered was "disruptive innovation."[7] There is even a competition for disruptive innovation, and a list of this year's most disruptive technologies in *Forbes* magazine.[8]

Disruptive innovation is a theory that propagates the notion that one organization outperforms another organization by producing a product that in turn puts the less desirable item out of business. The Church is not interested in disruptive innovation, and I don't believe that it is the best example of how life works. The Church is an organization that has lasted over thousands of years, and the future Church is even now becoming a transformed and transforming agent within the wider culture. It has had this longevity and will continue to adapt into the future, not because it is disrupted, dies, and something takes its place, but because it is a "dissipative" system that is constantly in touch with its environment and, therefore, ever adapting and changing in response to its mission context.[9]

Remember earlier we talked about Ilya Prigogine, who coined the phrase "dissipative structures," first putting forth the idea of *dissipation theory*.[10] This is the idea that the self-organizing system is changed, and transformed, as it interacts with its environment. Disorder disrupts and causes the organization, in turn, to experience a fluctuation, and adapt. We are not a cannibalizing organism that eats its own in order to manifest a new something. The present past Church is not destroyed by the future Church. Instead, here we have the metaphor of resurrection. Just as Jesus is bodily transformed in the resurrection, so the Church, as a dissipative organism, is transformed as it enters this new mission context. Some cells fall away, some cells stay, and some cells adapt and change. adding new colors and identity to the ever-growing and changing Church body.

This is important because the Church does not turn over one way of doing things, leave everyone behind, loot the organization, and move on. Just as the first disciples, facing the transition brought about by Pentecost and the new mission to the Gentiles, first took care of the widows and orphans, so too the Church is always mindful that it lives with many generations all together in one house. The Church today includes dear friends and mentors who invited me to consider ministry, but they are part of a Church that in many ways no longer exists. But the Church does not leave anyone behind. True, there are some who have departed and decided not to go along with us on this journey, and that makes me sad. But the Church has both the capacity and the responsibility to care for those who faithfully have supported the mission of the church in their age. It is perhaps for this reason that change and transformation within the organism is slow—at times painfully so.

Phyllis Tickle transformed the thinking of many when she offered her now essential text on the future Church entitled *The Great Emergence*.[11] In it she offers a history that highlights how every five hundred years the Church goes through a "rummage sale," cleaning out old forms of spirituality and replacing them with new ones. This does not mean that previous forms become obsolete or invalid. As in a dissipative organism, the old forms lose pride of place as the dominant driving forms, and new ones emerge as essential for navigating the mission context. She talks about Constantine in the fourth century, the Great Schism of the eleventh century, the Reformation in the sixteenth century, and now the post-modern era in the twenty-first century as points of reference for these changes. One can in fact go back further through the great history of the predecessor Jewish community, of which Christianity is a part, and see similar trends.

Tickle says that what is giving way right now is Protestantism, in the form that we know it, and what is appearing is a new form of Christianity, what she is calling "the Great Emergence." Tickle is not sure whether the new Christianity will emerge in a kind of tribal form, an individualistic form, a social form, or a combination of all of these. She is convinced that Protestantism in all its denominational forms is losing influence and is giving way to a disruptive form of Christian expression. It is difficult to imagine not having only one thing—Protestantism or something else. But my perspective, a postmodern one, tends to be at home with *both/and* visions of reality rather than *either/or* visions. I have no problem believing in and imagining a different future completely. The metanarrative has been deconstructed, and we have been living in a time of great fragmentation. Schrödinger's cat can be thought of as both alive and dead. Our Church can be seen as both dead and alive. The Episcopal Church can be both the Protestant Church of the past and the new Church of the future.

Tickle is right—the church is having a rummage sale. The present past Church is selling off the idea that uniformity is unity. It is selling off the idea that it is of value to the mission of the church that the second largest democratic meeting in the world (next to the parliament of India) is the Episcopal Church's General Convention. It is setting down its idea that liturgy must in all places be one. It is discarding the idea that sending money is all you have to do to make a difference in the world. It is shedding the mantle that Sunday morning attendance is the only requirement for good discipleship. It is selling off at a bargain basement price the notion that every church works on the same model, looks the same, and has the same ministries. It is letting go of the model of leadership that says one paid priest to one congregation. It is selling off the idea that a monthly paper newsletter counts as communication. It is setting aside the idea that mission is best funded through large bureaucratic institutions centralized for optimal control. It is, indeed, an immense rummage sale. Perhaps you will have some ideas about what else should be added to the list. At the end of the day all the refuse of the past Church will have to go, as the future Church is remade. One of the things that the

Gospels are clear about is that the fishermen immediately dropped their nets, they let go of their past, and they followed Jesus into their future. The future Church is making its pilgrim journey down the road to meet Jesus and lightening its load, casting off those things that hold it back from becoming the Kingdom of God.

I'd like to offer here a word of caution before we proceed about the future. I know that our "sense making machinery" wants to see the future just as it sees the past.[12] Our brains lead us to believe if we do x, y, and z, it will all work out. But we have no control over the future. The illusion that we do is comforting; our anxiety and fears may be assuaged if we just believe that if we do what we need to do, we will be all right in the end.[13] There is no guarantee, no matter how much our brain tells us this is good stuff and it will work. Businessmen and -women will try to beat the odds and illustrate how they outperformed everyone else. For the Christian, our task has been clear over the centuries: believe in God, believe in Jesus, believe in the power of the Holy Spirit to bring about the Kingdom of God, and believe that God's mission will be successful.

Accepting a new model of mission will inevitably bring a sense that this possible Church is the new normal—a new standard. We may be all too eager to say, "If you are not doing it this way then it isn't the future Church." This is exactly the kind of behavior that will shut down the creativity and life that is needed and sought. We need a lively conversation between traditions and versions of the Episcopal Church to remain energized. Instead of proclaiming that we all believe the same thing in the same way, the future Church will say, "Come along with us on this spiritual journey. We have a lot of questions, but God seems to be here in this stew, and we are all working hard to listen to the variety of voices God is using." The future Church is not a new standardized program, though it will be our tendency to make it so. It is not a way of taking away creativity and visions of what Church might be. This is not some new ministry offering a postmodern fundamentalism of futurist ideas.

The future Church is uncomfortable and chaotic. You may say that we don't have the wherewithal to accomplish it. You may say that we have shrunk beyond our ability to recover. Or, you may say we don't have enough funds. The Church has shown repeatedly its ability to adapt, create, and innovate without resources. It is not money or size that makes the difference.

Simon Sinek reminds us, in his important book *Start With Why*, that the Wright brothers had no support and no money, but they were focused on flight, and that is why they were the first to fly.[14] The leaders of tomorrow's Episcopal Church remember *why* we do what we do—God's mission of reconciliation. It is not money and it is not size or strength that drives us. It is our unity around the mission of God to reconcile himself to the world through acts of love that pulls us together to build a community that is at work in the world, serving and sharing the Good News of God in Christ Jesus. As Presiding Bishop Henry Knox Sherrill said in 1952, "The joyful news that He is risen does not change the contemporary world. Still before us lie work, discipline, sacrifice. But the fact of Easter gives us the spiritual power to do the work, accept the discipline, and make the sacrifice."[15]

This is the time to dream dreams. We would do well to remember the moment the Holy Spirit came down upon God's people.

> All were amazed and perplexed, saying to one another,
> "What does this mean?" But others sneered and said,
> "They are filled with new wine." And Peter said, "These
> are not drunk, as you suppose, for it is only nine o'clock
> in the morning. No, this is what was spoken through
> the prophet Joel: 'God declares, that I will pour out my
> Spirit upon all flesh, and your sons and your daughters
> shall prophesy, and your young men shall see visions,
> and your old men shall dream dreams.'"

Acts 2:12ff

This is not a time to stay small and on our island. This is not a time to remain sweet and precious. It is not a time to remain quiet. This is not a moment in which the church can or should work on legislating a pretty future. The future Episcopal Church needs people who get off the island and get messy in the world around us.

The future Church is depending on us to speak up and out. We are called to be bold. The future Church is hoping the present Church will engage the chaos around us. As we do this, we are going to have to be willing to mess up and do it wrong. It is okay to feel weak and it is okay to feel fear. People will ridicule us and people will try to shame us for daring greatly. But daring greatly is the call.

Daring greatly may be all there is. In the face of certain suffering, confusion, and even death—there is life. After all, daring greatly is the man on the cross. Daring greatly is resurrection. Daring greatly is the attitude of the future Church.[16] Brené Brown introduced me to this brilliant quote from Theodore Roosevelt. It reminds me that it is not those on the sidelines who make a difference.

> It is not the critic who counts; not the man who points out how the strong man stumbles, or where the doer of deeds could have done them better. The credit belongs to the man who is actually in the arena, whose face is marred by dust and sweat and blood; who strives valiantly; who errs, who comes short again and again, because there is no effort without error and shortcoming; but who does actually strive to do the deeds; who knows great enthusiasms, the great devotions; who spends himself in a worthy cause; who at the best knows in the end the triumph of high achievement, and who at the worst, if he fails, at least fails while daring greatly, so that his place shall never be with those cold and timid souls who neither know victory nor defeat.[17]

God is praying that laborers will go into the fields, for the harvest is great and laborers are few. Our call is to step forward as leaders committed to a future Church engaged in the mission of God. We are the ones to see the artifacts of the future Church around us today and to harness them for the missionary work of service and evangelism. We in the Episcopal Church must raise a loud shout and respond to God's prayer, affirming, "Our Church is alive! And, here I am, Lord, send me."

## Discussion Questions

1.  What excites you about the changes that Bishop Doyle advocates for in this book? What scares you about such "rummage sale" change?
2.  Bishop Doyle says that for the future Church to thrive, "the leadership must share information." What ideas, practices, and assumptions with respect to church leadership need to change for information to flow more freely throughout the organization?

3. Phyllis Tickle argues that the church is in the midst of having a rummage sale. What do you believe the Church most needs to get rid of? What do you believe needs to replace it?

4. Bishop Doyle is clear that "the Church does not leave anyone behind." As the future Church begins to emerge, who is most in danger of being left behind? What steps might we take to ensure that doesn't happen?

5. "This is the time to dream dreams." What is your most passionate dream for the Church? What can you do to help make that dream a reality?

## Spiritual Exercise

Bishop Doyle says that the Church "changes because that is the only way to preserve itself." Go online and watch this video in which Stanley Hauerwas offers an account of the Christian life (http://www. theworkofthepeople.com/what-is-a-christian). After doing so, reflect on how this video speaks to the church's task of embracing change as the necessary way of remain true to her unchanging task.

*Suggested Passage for Lectio Divina:* Mark 16:1–8

## Suggested Reading

Phyllis Tickle, *The Great Emergence: How Christianity Is Changing and Why.* Grand Rapids, MI: Baker Books, 2008.

Peter Senge, C. Otto Scharmer, Joseph Jaworski, and Betty Sue Flowers, *Presence: An Exploration of Profound Change in People, Organizations, and Society.* Boston: Nicholas Brealey, 2005.

# Appendix

## Lectio Divina

*Generous Community* will bear the most fruit when read, marked, and inwardly digested in the context of a small and generous community of people committed to cocreating the future Church with God. I believe that the work that God invites us to embrace is work that can only be done together in the context of an intentional contemplative practice of prayer and Scripture. That is why I have included a brief study guide at the end of each chapter that includes a recommended Bible passage to engage through a contemplative process called *lectio divina*.

*Lectio divina* means "divine reading." Rooted in traditional Benedictine practice, *lectio divina* is a specific form of Bible study that uses meditation and prayer to "experience" God's Word in a deep and mystical way. I invite you to study *Generous Community* with a small group of people and to encounter the recommended Bible passage that accompanies each chapter using the form of *lectio divina* outlined below.

Gather as a group and begin by observing a brief period of silence. This will set the tone for your contemplative reading.

Have someone pray the collect for Proper 28:

> Blessed Lord, who caused all holy Scriptures to be written
> for our learning: Grant us so to hear them, read, mark,
> learn, and inwardly digest them, that we may embrace
> and ever hold fast the blessed hope of everlasting life,

which you have given us in our Savior Jesus Christ; who lives and reigns with you and the Holy Spirit, one God, for ever and ever. Amen.[1]

One person reads the suggested passage slowly.

Each person identifies the word or phrase that grabs their attention.

Each shares the word or phrase with the other members of the group. No discussion, elaboration, or explanation is offered at this time.

Another person reads the passage a second time from a different translation.

Each person identifies where this passage touches his or her life today.

Each person shares with the group briefly.

The passage is read for the third time from a different translation.

Each person discerns, "From what I have heard and shared, what do I hear God inviting me to do or to be? In what aspect of my life and ministry is God inviting me to change?"

Each person shares their answer with the group.

The group then enters into prayer, with each person praying for the person to their right. The group then closes by praying the Lord's Prayer.

The steps above merely represent a suggested outline for structuring your *lectio divina* study. However, in the spirit of this book, we invite you to adventurously adapt, innovate, and to create your own.

# Notes

## Introduction

1. Bill Bryson, *At Home: A Short History of Private Life* (New York: Anchor Books, 2010), 7ff.

## 1. Schrödinger's Church

1. I first heard of Schrödinger's cat and superposition from Bill Bryson's book *A Short History of Nearly Everything* (New York: Random House, 2005), 191.
2. Ibid.
3. Margaret Wheatley, *Leadership and the New Science* (San Francisco: Berrett-Koehler, 2006), 68–70.
4. Paul Zahl, Episcopal Diocese of Texas Clergy Conference, 2012, on the doctrine of imputation.
5. Bob Johansen, *Leaders Make the Future* (San Francisco: Berrett-Koehler, 2012), 34.

## 2. A New Missionary Age

1. This image was first used in my Diocese of Texas Council Address in 2010. It was first published in my essay in the book *What We Shall Become: The Future and Structure of the Episcopal Church* (Church Publishing, 2013). It is expanded here.

2. Stephen E. Ambrose, *Undaunted Courage* (New York: Simon & Schuster, 1996), 266–67.

3. We cannot downplay the catastrophic collision about to take place between cultures, nor undertake some new kind of spiritual colonialism.

4. Bob Johansen, *Leaders Make the Future* (San Francisco: Berrett-Koehler, 2012), 6.

5. Judith Hicks Stiehm, *The U.S. Army War College* (Philadelphia: Temple University Press, 2002), 6.

6. Bob Johansen, *Get There Early* (San Francisco: Berrett-Koehler, 2007), 51–53.

7. Two authors, Margaret Wheatley and Marina Gorbis, survey the world around us and see that our culture is filled with organizations that are using outdated models of community life to find their way in the emerging millennia in which we find ourselves. See Wheatley, *Leadership and the New Science* (San Francisco: Berrett-Koehler, 2006) and Gorbis, *The Nature of the Future* (New York: Free Press, 2013).

8. Wheatley, 7.

9. Thomas Friedman, *The World Is Flat* (New York: Farrar, Straus & Giroux, 2005).

10. Gorbis, 99.

11. Barna Group, "New Statistics on Church Attendance and Avoidance," March 3, 2008, www.barna.org/barna-update/congregations/45-new-statistics-on-church-attendance-and-avoidance. "Unattached—people who had attended neither a conventional church nor an organic faith community (e.g., house church, simple church, intentional community) during the past year. Some of these people use religious media, but they have had no personal interaction with a regularly convened faith community. This segment represents one out of every four adults (23%) in America. About one-third of the segment was people who have never attended a church at any time in their life."

12. The Apostle Paul was a tentmaker and an evangelist. A popular way of referring to clergy who make their living at a different job from working full time for the church is "tentmaker."

13. The Rt. Rev. Ian Douglas is the first person I heard use this phrase, "God has a mission, God's mission has a church."

## 3. A Courageous Church

1. Adapted from Brené Brown, *Daring Greatly* (New York: Gotham Books, 2012), 63.
2. Ibid., 64.
3. Ibid., 65. Adapted from a quote from Peter Sheahan.
4. Ibid., 65.
5. Ibid., 64.
6. Bob Johansen, *Leaders Make the Future* (San Francisco: Berrett-Koehler, 2012), 50.
7. Ibid.
8. Ibid., 51.
9. Augustine of Hippo, *The Confessions* (Grand Rapids, MI: Baker Book House, 2005), 216ff.
10. Bob Johansen, *Get There Early* (San Francisco: Berrett-Koehler, 2007), 21.
11. Institute for the Future, "2008–2018 Map of Future Forces Affecting the Episcopal Church" (presented at the Consortium of Endowed Parishes meeting at St. David's Episcopal Church, Austin, Texas, 2008).
12. Bob Johansen explains these ideas well in *Leaders Make the Future*. These ideas are also present in Guy Kawasaki and Clay Shirky's work.
13. Margaret Wheatley, *Leadership and the New Science* (San Francisco: Berrett-Koehler, 2006), 12.
14. Ibid.
15. Nassim Nicholas Taleb, *Antifragile: Things That Gain from Disorder* (New York: Random House, 2012), 151.
16. Johansen, *Leaders*, 32.

## 4. Our Guiding Principles

1. Milton Richardson was the fifth bishop diocesan of Texas.
2. Book of Common Prayer, 867.
3. George Barna and Mark Hatch, *Boiling Point: Monitoring Cultural Shifts in the 21st Century* (Ventura, CA: Regal Books, 2001), 17ff.
4. I do not imply here a neo-latitudinarianism. I believe this freedom is only manifest within a community that proclaims

a monotheistic faith in God as creator and Jesus as the incarnate Son who fulfills salvation history. It is only without faith in a Trinitarian God and the basics of the faith that you get latitudinarianism—that is, those who offer the practice of religion without doctrine.

5. Book of Common Prayer, 858.
6. Book of Common Prayer, 360.
7. Alexander Schmemann, *For the Life of the World* (Crestwood, NY: St. Vladimir's Seminary Press, 1973), 99.
8. "Political Polarization and Personal Life," Pew Research Center, June 12, 2014, www.people-press.org/2014/06/12/section-3-political-polarization-and-personal-life/.
9. Wendell Berry, "It All Turns on Affection," Awards and Honors: 2012 Jefferson Lecture, www.neh.gov/about/awards/jefferson-lecture/wendell-e-berry-lecture.
10. Marina Gorbis, *The Nature of the Future* (New York: Free Press, 2013), 176.
11. Thom Rainer, "Seven Reasons Why Church Worship Centers Will Get Smaller," December 9, 2013, thomrainer.com/2013/12/09/seven-reasons-why-church-worship-centers-will-get-smaller/. See also Ed Stetzer, "Starting, Staffing, and Supporting a Multisite Church," *Christianity Today*, March 17, 2014, www.christianitytoday.com/edstetzer/2014/march/starting-staffing-and-supporting-multisite-church.html; Tim Nations, "What 7 Rapidly Growing Churches Are Learning About Multisite," Leadnet, May 15th, 2014, leadnet.org/what-7-rapidly-growing-churches-are-learning-about-multisite/; and Adelle M. Banks, "Vitality in Multisite Church Model," Religion News Service, March 11, 2014, www.washingtonpost.com/national/religion/survey-finds-growth-vitality-in-multisite-church-model/2014/03/11/7affef86-a944-11e3-8a7b-c1c684e2671f_story.html.
12. Leadership Network, "Leadership Network/Generis Multisite Church Scorecard," leadnet.org/wp-content/uploads/2014/03/2014_LN_Generis_Multisite_Church_Scorecard_Report_v2.pdf.
13. Institute for the Future, "The Internet Human," www.iftf.org/internethuman/.
14. Ibid.
15. Institute for the Future, "2008 Map of the Decade," www.iftf.org/our-work/global-landscape/ten-year- forecast/2008-map-of-the-decade/.
16. Ibid.

168

## 5. Autopoietic Communities

1. Fritjof Capra, *The Turning Point* (New York: Bantam, 1983), 76–77. As quoted in Margaret Wheatley, *Leadership and the New Science* (San Francisco: Berrett-Koehler, 2006), 3, 5–6.
2. Wheatley, 5ff.
3. Werner Heisenberg, *Physics and Philosophy: The Revolution in Modern Science* (New York: Harper, 1958).
4. Werner Heisenberg, "Critique of the Physical Concepts of the Corpuscular Theory," in *The Physical Principles of the Quantum Theory*, Carl Eckhart and Frank C. Hoyt, trans. (1930), 20.
5. I learned this from Daniel Kahneman in his Nobel Prize-winning text on economics, *Thinking, Fast and Slow* (New York: Farrar, Straus and Giroux, 2011), and from Nassim Nicholas Taleb in his magnum opus *Antifragile: Things That Gain from Disorder* (New York: Random House, 2012).
6. Kahneman, 201.
7. Wheatley, 6.
8. Bill Bryson, *At Home: A Short History of Private Life* (New York: Anchor Books, 2010), 25.
9. Wheatley, 101ff.
10. Ibid.
11. Nassim Nicholas Taleb, *Black Swan* (New York: Random House, 2007), 8.
12. A Procrustean bed is a standard that is enforced uniformly without regard to individuality. Procrustes was a mythological figure who cut people down to size to fit in an iron bed.
13. Taleb, 106.
14. Kahneman, 85–87.
15. Ibid., 202.
16. Wayne Meeks, *First Urban Christians* (New Haven, CT: Yale University Press, 1983), 76–83. Much of this section is based on this book.
17. Edward Foley, *From Age to Age: How Christians Have Celebrated the Eucharist* (Chicago: Liturgy Training Publications, 1991), 39. The customary is a list of usual practices for a community.
18. Ibid., 63.
19. Ibid., 87.
20. Bryson, 322, 475ff.

21. Charles Taylor, *A Secular Age* (Cambridge, MA: Belknap Press of Harvard University Press, 2007), 775.
22. Ibid., 774.
23. Ibid., 542.
24. Ibid., 543.
25. Harvey Cox, *Religion in the Secular City: Toward a Postmodern Theology* (New York: Simon and Schuster: New York, 1984), 159.
26. If you are interested in further reading the following texts are suggested: *The In-Between Church* (Bethesda, MD: The Alban Institute, 1998); contributions by Dan Hotchkiss to the article, "Searching for the Key: Developing a Theory of Synagogue Size," *Congregations* 27, no. 1 (January–February 2001); a recent work by Gary McIntosh, *One Size Doesn't Fit All* (Grand Rapids, MI: Revell, 1999); and some preliminary findings from the National Congregations Study (NCS) headed by Mark Chaves. "The tipping point" has become a household term because of Malcolm Gladwell's book, *The Tipping Point: How Little Things Can Make a Big Difference* (Boston: Little, Brown, 2000).
27. Arlin Rothauge, *Sizing Up Your Congregation* (New York: Seabury Professional Services, 1986). Available at www.episcopalchurch.org/files/CDR_series1(1).pdf.
28. Wheatley, 65.
29. Margaret Wheatley, *Finding Our Way* (San Francisco: Berrett-Koehler, 2005), 68.
30. Ibid.
31. Ibid.
32. Capra, *Turning Point*, 96, 99. As quoted in Wheatley, *New Science*, 20.
33. Wheatley, *New Science*, 34.

# 6. A Renewed Mission Field

1. "Smart Cities and Smart Citizens." *Sustain*, sustainmagazine.com/smart-cities-smart-citizens (May 1, 2013).
2. June Williamson, "Urban Design Tactics for Suburban Retrofitting," Build A Better Burb, buildabetterburb.org/11-urban-design-tactics-for-suburban-retrofitting/.
3. Ibid.

4. Ellen Dunham-Jones and June Williamson, *Retrofitting Suburbia: Urban Design Solutions for Redesigning Suburbs* (New York: Wiley, 2011).

5. "Domestic Racial and Ethnic Membership Report for 2009," Episcopal Church, archive.episcopalchurch.org/research/109378_106716_ENG_HTM.htm.

6. William P. Hall and Susu Nousala, "Autopoiesis and Knowledge in Self-Sustaining Organizational Systems," 4th International Multiconference on Society, Cybernetics and Informatics, June 2010, Orlando, FL. This paper challenges the idea that there is ever a closed system sociologically or molecularly. Systems are always porous to their surroundings. Much of this section is based on this paper. It is available at www.academia.edu/6376323/Proceedings_of_the_4th_International_Multi-Conference_on_Society_Cybernetics_and_Informatics_IMSCI_2010_Vol._2.

7. Ibid.

8. Ibid. See the RAND report here: www.rand.org/content/dam/rand/pubs/research_memoranda/2006/RM3764.pdf.

9. Hall and Nousala.

10. Stuart Brand, "Founding Father," *Wired*, September 2003, archive.wired.com/wired/archive/9.03/baran_pr.html.

11. Ibid.

12. George Barna and Mike Hatch, *Boiling Point: How Coming Cultural Shifts Will Change Your Life* (Grand Rapids, MI: Baker Books, 2001), 250. Some of the trends in this section are based on this book.

13. Barna and Hatch, 25. The Barna Group calls these Boutique Churches: "These are congregations with one ministry: worship, discipleship, fellowship, community service."

14. Learn more about Episcopal Service Corps at episcopalservicecorps.org.

15. Barna and Hatch, 252.

16. Margaret Wheatley, *Leadership and the New Science* (San Francisco: Berrett-Koehler, 2006), 20.

17. Ibid.

18. Ibid., 21. Wheatley is getting her information from the landmark paper by Prigogine and Stengers, published in 1984.

19. Ibid., 4.

# 7. Into the Cloud of Unknowing

1. I think it is important to point out that Sheldon Cooper of *The Big Bang Theory* named his cats after all the members of the Manhattan Project, including Feynman. One he named Zazzles because he was "so zazzy." I also have a cat named Zazzles. Episode entitled *The Zazzy Substitution*, http://bigbangtheory.wikia.com/wiki/Sheldon's_Cats.
2. John Carl Villanueva, "Electron Cloud Model," Universe Today, August 25, 2009, http://www.universetoday.com/38282/electron-cloud-model/#ixzz33vq8ipk1. While thinking about how to begin this chapter, the Rev. Patrick Miller and I were at the Latin church site in the Holy Land where they remember the Ascension of Jesus. He mentioned in passing that quantum physicists used clouds as a way of describing their work. So I looked it up.
3. Ibid.
4. *The Cloud of Unknowing and Other Works*, trans. A. C. Spearing (New York: Penguin Classics, 2001), chapter 6.
5. Nassim Nicholas Taleb, *Antifragile: Things that Gain from Disorder* (New York: Random House, 2012), 32.
6. Ibid.
7. Casuistry is the application of theoretical rules to particular situations.
8. Taleb, 26.
9. Optionality is the multiplicity of investment opportunities that only come after the initial investment.

# 8. Communities of Service

1. Book of Common Prayer, 302ff.
2. See Dambisa Moyo, *Dead Aid: Why Aid Is Not Working and How There Is a Better Way for Africa* (New York: Farrar, Straus & Giroux, 2009).
3. Robert Lupton, *Toxic Charity: How Churches and Charities Hurt Those They Help, and How to Reverse It* (San Francisco: HarperOne, 2011), 5. Much of this section is informed by Lupton's book, with quotations cited.
4. Ibid., 34.
5. Ibid., 8.

6. Ibid., 139.
7. Marina Gorbis, *The Nature of the Future* (New York: Free Press, 2013), 29.
8. Bradley Kreit, "Investing in Local Communities to Improve Health," Institute for the Future, November 7, 2011, http://member.iftf.org/node/3989.
9. Ibid.
10. These goals are taken from a yearlong study of how to reinvigorate service ministry in health in the Diocese of Texas. Visioning, research, and community study led the staff and board of the Episcopal Health Foundation to adopt this broad framework. I believe it is a hallmark of defining the future of service that truly meets real need in our communities.
11. Adapted from the Episcopal Health Foundation Strategic Plan.
12. Jonathan Lerner, "Pop-Up Urbanism to Build Community Health: Street Makeovers Put New Spin on the Block," *Pacific Magazine*: The Science of Society, January 16, 2012, http://www.psmag.com/magazines/news-and-options/street-makeovers-put-new-spin-on-the-block-38926/.
13. Ibid.
14. See www.betterblock.org.
15. "Complete streets," Wikipedia, http://en.wikipedia.org/wiki/Complete_streets.
16. See www.macro-sea.org.
17. Lerner, "Pop-Up Urbanism."
18. See chapter 6, Our Guiding Principles.
19. See houstonrevision.org.

## 9. Generous Evangelism

1. Bob Johansen, *Leaders Make the Future* (San Francisco: Berrett-Koehler, 2012), 55.
2. Rodney Stark, *The Rise of Christianity: A Sociologist Reconsiders History* (Princeton, NJ: Princeton University Press, 1996), as quoted by ChurchHistory.net, *Christianity Today*. These estimates are based on 40 percent growth per decade, and roughly correspond with figures found in early church documents. See http://www.christianitytoday.com/ch/1998/issue57/57h026.html.

3. Richard D. Balge, "A Brief History of Evangelism in the Christian Church" (Synod-Wide Convocation on Evangelism, Wisconsin Lutheran College, Milwaukee, Wisconsin, 1978). Available at www.wlsessays.net/node/34. Much of the history in this section is based on this essay.

4. Ibid.

5. For more on "generous evangelism," hear the author's series of evangelism lectures given in November 2011. Available at www.adoyle.libsyn.com/webpage/2011/11 (follow the Direct download link).

6. Guy Kawasaki, "The Art of Evangelism," January 12, 2006. See guykawasaki.com/the_art_of_evan/.

7. Ibid.

8. Richard Ruff, "Active listening—a forgotten key to sales success," Sales Training Connection, September 16, 2011, http://salestraining connection.com/2011/09/16/active-listening-a-forgotten-key-to-sales-success. The ideas in the paragraph are summed up well in the above article. I learned most of this in Clinical Pastoral Education and in Transformative Mediation training at George Mason. This is a good short article on the basics.

9. Ibid.

# 10. The Future of Stewardship

1. That is correct—the separation of Church and State was not normative until 1833. The Constitution is referring to a national church, but at the time it was assumed that local churches would be supported by the government for their charity work.

2. Charles Ryrie, *Balancing the Christian Life* (Chicago: Moody Press, 1994), 86.

3. Scott Bader-Saye, "Bonds of Affection: The Transformational Possibilities of a Platitude," The Conference, Diocese of Texas, 2014.

4. Wendell E. Berry, "It All Turns on Affection," 2012 Jefferson Lecture, National Endowment for the Humanities. Available at http://www.neh.gov/about/awards/jefferson-lecture/wendell-e-berry-lecture.

5. Jerry Michalski, "Thriving in the Relationship Economy," Institute for the Future, August 31, 2013, http://prezi.com/3igqdq90g-y0/thriving-in-the-relationship-economy/.

6. Robert D. Lupton, *Toxic Charity: How Churches and Charities Hurt Those They Help, and How to Reverse It* (San Francisco: HarperOne, 2011).
7. Marina Gorbis, *The Nature of the Future* (New York: Free Press, 2013), 60.
8. Ibid.
9. "Research and Statistics," Episcopal Church, http://www.episcopal church.org/page/research-and-statistics.
10. Clay Shirkey, *Cognitive Surplus: Creativity and Curiosity in a Connected Age* (New York: Penguin, 2010), 4–5.
11 Gorbis, 64.

# 11. Generous Community

1. Sue Mallory, *The Equipping Church: Serving Together to Transform Lives* (Grand Rapids, MI: Zondervan, 2001).
2. John Newton, "Front-door Evangelism Theology," Resources for Invite-Welcome-Connect, Episcopal Diocese of Texas, http://www.epicenter.org/newcomer.
3. "Vision Statement," Diocese of Texas, http://www.epicenter.org/diocese/about-the-diocese/vision.
4. "The Future of Persuasion," Institute for the Future, Summer 2010, http://www.iftf.org/uploads/media/SR-1321_IFTF_FutureofPersuasion Report-1.pdf. Much of this section is based on this report.
5. Ibid.
6. Ibid.
7. Ibid.

# 12. Self-Forming Creative Christians

1. Verna J. Dozier, *The Dream of God: A Call to Return* (Cambridge, MA: Cowley Publications, 1991), 67.
2. John Newton, *New Clothes* (New York: Church Publishing, 2014), 137.
3. I am adapting here ideas from Sir Ken Robinson's TED talk on the future of education to highlight how creativity will play a key role in our work of formation. Ken Robinson, TED Talk, http://blog.ted.com/2006/06/27/sir_ken_robinso/.

4. Ibid.
5. Knowledge Tools of the Future," IFTF, 2008, http://www.iftf. org/our-work/people-technology/technology-horizons/knowledge-tools-of-the-future/.
6. Vannevar Bush, "As We May Think," *Atlantic Monthly*, July 1, 1945, http://www.theatlantic.com/magazine/archive/1945/07/as-we-may-think/303881/.
7. Marina Gorbis, *The Nature of the Future* (New York: Free Press, 2013), 161.
8. John Naisbitt, *Megatrends* (New York: Time Warner Books, 1982), 32ff.
9. Christoper T. Hill, "The Post Scientific Society," *Issues in Science and Technology*, Fall 2007, 78–84.
10. Ross Mayfield, "Web of Verbs," Ross Mayfield's Weblog, http://ross.typepad.com/blog/2005/08/web_of_verbs.html.
11. Ibid.
12. Ross Mayfield, "Weblog: Market's Technology & Musings," October 13, 2008, http://ross.typepad.com/blog/2005/08/web_of_verbs.html.
13. The section that follows is informed by "Extreme Learners," Institute for the Future, 2014. See http://www.iftf.org/our-work/global-landscape/learning/extreme-learners/.
14. "Learning: 2020 Forecast," Institute for the Future, 2013, http://www.iftf.org/our-work/global-landscape/learning/.
15. Gorbis, 83.
16. "Learning: 2020 Forecast."
17. Gorbis, 91. I am adapting a Gorbis quote regarding the future of education: "Social structured education actually brings us back to a future envisioned by Socrates, Rousseau, and Dewey, but with a whole new set of tools. . . . These tools and platforms make it possible for us to pursue education that is individually paced and intrinsically motivated. We can use these tools to make the dream of Socrates, Rousseau, and Dewey a reality. We can create the kind of rich, meaningful, de-institutionalized education they envisioned."

# 13. Making Change

1. Adapted from Margaret Wheatley, *Finding Our Way* (San Francisco: Berrett-Koehler, 2007), 84.

2. Ibid., 89.
3. Ibid., 91.
4. Adapted from Marina Gorbis, *The Nature of the Future* (New York: Free Press, 2013), 199.
5. Ibid.
6. Ibid., 157.
7. Jill Lepore, "Disruption Machine: What the Gospel of Innovation Gets Wrong," *New Yorker*, June 23, 2014.
8. Paul Nunes and Larry Downes, "The Five Most Disruptive Innovations," *Forbes*, January 10, 2014, http://www.forbes.com/sites/bigbangdisruption/2014/01/10/the-five-most-disruptive-innovations-at-ces-2014/.
9. Margaret Wheatley, *Leadership and the New Science* (San Francisco: Berrett-Koehler, 2006), 21.
10. Simon Sinek, Ilya Prigogine and Isabelle Stengers, *Order out of Chaos* (New York: Bantam Books, 1984). As quoted in Wheatley, 21.
11. Phyllis Tickle, *The Great Emergence: How Christianity Is Changing and Why* (Grand Rapids, MI: Baker Books, 2008).
12. Daniel Kahneman, *Thinking Fast and Slow* (New York: Faarrar, Straus, and Giroux, 2011), 204.
13. Ibid.
14. Simon Sinek, *Start with Why: How Great Leaders Inspire Everyone to Take Action* (New York: Portfolio, 2009), 11ff.
15. Henry Knox Sherrill, "Easter Address," *Outlook*, March 1952.
16. Brené Brown, *Daring Greatly* (New York: Gotham Books, 2012), 59ff. Adapted.
17. Excerpt from Theodore Roosevelt's speech "Citizenship in a Republic," delivered at the Sorbonne, in Paris, France, on April 23, 1910, http://www.theodore-roosevelt.com/images/research/speeches/maninthearena.pdf. Brené Brown first introduced me to this speech in *Daring Greatly*.

# Appendix

1. Proper 28 can be found on page 236 of the Book of Common Prayer. It is reproduced here for your convenience, but the Book of Common Prayer should always be close at hand.

CPSIA information can be obtained
at www.ICGtesting.com
Printed in the USA
LVOW11s0015260917

550043LV00001B/149/P